INCREDIBLE CATS

Every feline, from the most aristocratic Siamese to the humblest tabby, possesses powers so remarkable that they are not to be found in any other animal on earth. Behind those soulful eyes and soft coats lurk the spirits of wild ancestors—spirits which endow even the most apparently placid and domesticated of cats with unique and mysterious abilities.

I have been studying these powers for more than ten years. I have talked to owners, interviewed breeders and observed researchers engaged in the difficult, often frustrating, task of finding scientific explanations for many of this extraordinary creature's more improbable accomplishments. My purpose in writing the book is to share with you all I have discovered about the secret life of these amazing animals.

YOUR INCREDIBLE CAT

Understanding the Secret Powers of Your Pet

David Greene

IVY BOOKS · NEW YORK

Ivy Books
Published by Ballantine Books
Copyright © 1984 by David Greene

Library of Congress Catalog Card Number: 85-27375

ISBN-0-8041-0139-6

This edition published by arrangement with Doubleday & Company, Inc.

Manufactured in the United States of America

First Ballantine Books Edition: October 1987

Line drawings by Richard Armstrong.

To

Pudden, a discerning and affectionate friend,
and
Shirlee and Leroy, two handsome Burmese
who were such a help in my researches

Contents

CHAPTER 1

Incredible Cats

Watching your cat at work or play, marveling at his quick intelligence and enchanted by his elegant grace, you may have been tempted to think—"He's almost human."*

But you would have been wrong, for cats are not so much human as superhuman!

Every feline, from the most aristocratic Siamese to the humblest tabby, possesses powers so remarkable that they are not to be found in any other animal on earth. Behind those soulful eyes and soft coats lurk the spirits of wild ancestors from whom the present-day pet is descended— spirits which endow even the most apparently placid and domesticated of cats with unique and mysterious abilities.

I have been studying these powers for more than ten

---

*For the sake of convenience, I shall refer to the cat as "he" unless talking about a specific cat who is female. This should certainly not be taken to imply that male cats are in any way superior to females.

years in a quest which has taken me around the world. I have talked to owners, interviewed breeders and watched researchers engaged in the difficult, and often frustrating, task of finding scientific explanations for many of this extraordinary creature's more improbable accomplishments.

I have met some of the world's most valuable and pampered pets as they dined from gold plates in elegant penthouse suites under the watchful gaze of armed bodyguards. And I have also accompanied animal welfare workers on their rescue missions around the rubbish-littered alleys of the city slums as they fought to save abandoned strays from starvation, sickness and death.

My purpose in writing this book is to share with you, probably a cat owner but almost certainly a cat lover, all I have discovered about the secret life of these amazing animals, including the powers which enable cats to:

- use extrasensory perception to predict danger to themselves, their companions and their owners;
- perform intellectually demanding tasks so difficult that many humans could not accomplish them;
- give early warning of natural disasters;
- cure apparently hopeless cases of mental and physical illness;
- save people from apparently inescapable injury or death;
- track down their owners across thousands of miles;
- survive accidents that would spell certain death to almost any other creature;
- communicate eloquently, with other animals and humans, by means of a complex language of sounds, movements and odors.

After reading this book I am sure you will agree with

me that, far from exaggerating their potential, the description "Incredible Cats" hardly does them justice.

Three of the many stories from my research files vividly illustrate a few of these powers in action. The first concerns a part-Persian her owner named Sugar. But the newspapers which reported her exploits came up with a far more fitting title. In banner headlines across the nation they called her "Supercat."

Sugar—The Cat That Crossed Half a Continent

Sugar was born in the small California town of Anderson on the Sacramento River. A weakly kitten, she had an unusual deformity in her left hip bone. It was this disability which later helped to provide the vital confirmation of her identity and so gave her a place in the cats' hall of fame.

When Sugar was two, her owner, Mary, moved from Anderson to a new home in Oklahoma, some 1,500 miles away. The journey had to be made by car, and knowing that Sugar loathed even the shortest trip, Mary came to the reluctant conclusion that it would be kinder to leave her pet behind. A good home was found with a kindly neighbor and Mary said a tearful goodbye. But Sugar, though comfortably settled, had no intention of being abandoned. Two weeks later, a phone call from the neighbor brought Mary sad news. Her pet had vanished and, despite all intensive search, no trace of her could be found.

As the weeks and months went by without further news, Mary reluctantly accepted that Sugar must be dead. Fourteen months later, as she worked in her garden, a familiar half-Persian cat suddenly appeared and made its way wearily across the lawn toward her.

For a moment woman and cat just stared at one another, Mary in amazement, the cat with what might have been a glint of triumph in her gaze. Then, with a meow of delight, Sugar bounded across the grass and, giving little hops of welcome, rubbed herself affectionately against her mistress's legs.

The cat was exhausted but otherwise in excellent condition, needing only a fish supper and a good night's rest to restore her to perfect health. After walking halfway across the United States, Sugar had somehow managed to locate the right house in the right street of the right town.

At first Mary's friends were, not surprisingly, extremely skeptical of the story. But when an examination of the cat's left hip revealed the same unique bone deformity, no doubts remained. Somehow—and none of the animal experts I have talked to can offer any completely satisfactory explanation for the feat—Sugar had successfully trailed her owner halfway across a continent.

Although Sugar's powers are remarkable, they are by no means unique. We shall be looking at accounts of equally amazing journeys later in the book, and also seeing what progress science is making in discovering exactly how cats are capable of such apparently impossible achievements.

The second story is one whose happy ending was only possible thanks to some kind of feline ESP.

Sticky—The Cat in the Bag

Tom and Sticky were born on a farm outside the West Country town of Okehampton, England. Tom was a distinguished black-and-white cat, a sturdy animal who, even as a kitten, was a fearless explorer. Sticky, the runt of the litter, got her name from thin, sticklike legs. As a kitten she was frightened of everything and, even though she grew slightly bolder as time went by, Sticky remained a timid creature.

Tom and Sticky stayed on at the farm after the rest of the litter had been found homes, and soon became inseparable companions. While Tom prowled the countryside with all the pride of an undisputed monarch, the faithful Sticky trotted loyally along at his side. Together they roamed the fields and pastures, hunted mice around the farm and slept side-by-side in the barn.

Then the farmer died and Alice, his widow, moved to the town of Newton Abbot. Because her new house was rather small, it was only possible to keep one of the cats and she chose Tom—always her favorite.

Sticky was given to her sister Joyce, who lived in Plymouth, so, after years of companionship, the two friends finally parted. One morning, about eight months after the move, Alice noticed that Tom appeared unusually agitated. Instead of sleeping in his favorite corner by the fire, the cat was restlessly pacing the room, ears flattened and erect tail flicking from side to side (powerful silent speech signals of annoyance, as we shall see in Chapter Three). Suddenly he launched himself with terrifying ferocity against the door, his claws tearing at the woodwork and leaving deep scratches in the paint.

Bewildered, and unable to calm him down, Alice phoned her sister for advice. But when Joyce came on the line it was to report problems of her own. Tearfully, she told her sister that Sticky had disappeared from home earlier the same morning. A neighbor claimed to have seen the terrified cat being chased down the street by a gang of youths, but despite a search no sign of the animal could be found.

"I'll drive over and help you look," said Alice, her own difficulties with Tom immediately forgotten. She intended to leave the cat at home, but no sooner was the back door opened than he raced past her legs to the car. Because she was in such a hurry, Alice decided to take Tom with her. Later she was to be thankful that she had.

When they reached Plymouth, Tom leaped out and ran down the street, taking absolutely no notice of Alice's frantic cries. At the corner, however, he paused and turned to stare at her, tail flicking urgently. Alice called her sister and the two women set off in pursuit. The cat led them through a maze of side streets, never faltering and only pausing from time to time so that they could keep up.

Finally, as they reached a patch of vacant land, close to the harbor, Tom vanished from sight. It was only his loud and excited meowing that enabled Alice and Joyce to trace him to a dank underground chamber, part of an old wartime shelter. The gloomy interior was stacked with the accumulated rubbish of years. But Tom had not hesitated. He was frantically scratching at a large burlap sack whose neck was tightly bound with twine. As Alice and Joyce stared in horror, the sack moved slightly. Something was trapped inside it.

That something was Sticky. She had been roughly treated by her captors before being tossed into the bag and left as dead. Thanks to the skill of a local vet and patient nursing by Alice, Sticky was restored to health, and after that the sisters decided that Tom and Sticky belonged together, so they were reunited. When I visited them at their comfortable home, the pair was curled together by a fire—the picture of feline contentment.

Neither Alice nor Joyce can explain how Tom apparently knew of his sister's anguish, nor how he was able to find her so easily in a strange city.

Do cats really have nine lives? The question is posed, and perhaps answered, by my final story.

Jacob—The Cat Who Lived Underwater

On a pitch-black and bitterly cold night in December 1964, the Dutch vessel *Tjoba* was making her way cautiously down the River Rhine. Suddenly there was a violent collision; the *Tjoba* heeled over and, almost immediately, started to sink. Within minutes she was on the bottom, leaving her crew splashing for their lives in the freezing water. All were saved, but there still seemed to be one casualty. Jacob, the ship's six-year-old cat, had been trapped below deck and gone down with the vessel. It was eight days later that giant cranes were maneuvered into position above the wreckage to carry out the laborious task of raising the wreck and clearing the waterway of its obstruction. Divers attached chains, winches took the strain and the remains of the vessel were slowly raised from the mud of the riverbed.

When the *Tjoba* had finally been brought to the surface, the crew was allowed aboard to save what they could of their waterlogged belongings. As he pushed open his cabin door, the captain started back in amazement. Jacob, shivering with cold and extremely hungry, came hurrying over to beg for food. He had survived more than a week underwater in a bubble of trapped air!

How the Long Relationship Began

There have been wild cats in Europe, Asia and Africa for many thousands of years, but it was a long while before man decided that here was an animal worth domesticating. Although it is impossible to state exactly when this was achieved, we do know that Egyptians used cats to guard their granaries against rodents more than two thousand years before the birth of Christ.

Respect for the cat's powers quickly changed to veneration and the animal was made sacred to Isis or the moon. It was worshipped with great ceremony as a moon symbol not only because the animal is more active after sunset, but because, with the dilation and constriction of its pupils, a cat's eyes seem to reflect the moon's own waxing and waning. The cat was also the sacred animal of the goddess Diana, the daughter of Isis and the sister of Horus, the Sun God. Diana, who represented the sun's life-giving heat, was depicted as having the head of a cat, perhaps from that creature's fondness for basking in the sun.

From Egypt the cat made its way to Rome and became the symbol of liberty. Statues of the Goddess of Liberty show her holding a cup in one hand and a broken scepter in the other, with a cat, that least restrained of all domesticated animals, lying at her feet.

From Rome the cat marched with the conquering legions across the length and breadth of vanquished Europe. Exactly when the animal arrived in Britain is not known, although the unmistakable imprints of cat paws have been found on tiles excavated from the Roman towns of Silchester and Uriconium. It appears that the workmen had just put the tiles out to dry when a cat wandered across them and left an indelible pawprint in history. When archaeologists started to unearth the remains of a Roman villa at Lullingstone, destroyed by fire around A.D. 200, the skeleton of a cat, almost certainly a family pet, was found amidst the blackened ruins.

Today, some 4,000 years since cats and humans started sharing hearth and home, the pet is as popular as ever. Indeed, so eager are many people to own the "ideal" animal that special breeding techniques are being employed to create a race of "custom cats." Top establishments such as Fabulous Felines and Prestige Pets of New York now produce cats precisely tailored to satisfy a demanding clientele. For around $400 you can now purchase a Himalayan, claimed by its breeders to be the world's friendliest and most affectionate cat. The breed, half Siamese and half Persian, with Siamese markings on a Persian coat, is notable for its warm, friendly nature, liking nothing better than to sit for hours on an owner's lap being petted. And for those who prefer kittens to cats, Prestige Pets also offers Mini Himalayans, guaranteed never to grow bigger than a four-month-old kitten. This is achieved by breeding from the runt of the litter over many succeeding generations.

But although the long association between mankind and cats has been close and, for much of the time, mutually beneficial, it has not always been an especially happy partnership for the pet. For a unique feature of this relationship is the intensity of feelings which are aroused. Where cats are concerned, there appear to be no half measures: you either love them or loathe them.

Famous cat-lovers have included the author Raymond Chandler, Sir Winston Churchill, Albert Schweitzer and the prophet Mohammed. Raymond Chandler talked to his black Persian, Taki, as though she was human and jokingly called her his secretary because she sat on manuscripts as he tried to revise them. Churchill's cat, Jock, shared both his master's bed and his supper table. The war leader often sent servants to find Jock and refused to start eating until his cat was present. While working in Africa, Schweitzer—who was left-handed—sometimes wrote prescriptions with his right hand so as not to disturb his cat, Sizi, who liked to fall asleep on his left arm. Mohammed considered dogs unclean but approved of cats. On one occasion he cut off the sleeve of a robe to avoid awakening a sleeping cat as he rose to pray.

But cats have also had their equally distinguished detractors, including the composer Johannes Brahms, Napoleon Bonaparte, Noah Webster and Dwight D. Eisenhower. When not at the keyboard, Brahms's favorite form of relaxation seems to have been sitting at an open window and attempting, usually with success, to kill neighborhood cats with a bow and arrow. During one campaign, an aide to Napoleon was startled by the emperor calling loudly for assistance. Opening the door, he discovered his master half-naked, sweating with fear and lunging wildly with his sword at the tapestry-covered walls. The cause of his terror—a small kitten! In his famous dictionary, Webster had little good to say for the cat, which he described as a "deceitful animal and when enraged extremely spiteful." And Eisenhower's loathing for cats was so great that he gave his staff orders to shoot any seen on the grounds of his Gettysburg home.

These extreme personal views mirror social attitudes toward cats. For although there have been periods of human history in which they were worshipped as gods, there have also been times during which cats were tortured as demons or slaughtered in macabre acts of symbolic rebellion.

When a cat died in ancient Egypt it was buried with full pomp and ritual, and while Egyptians, in common with many other societies of that age, occasionally showed mercy over the slaying of another human, killing—or in some cases simply injuring—a cat, even by accident, was punished by death.

Compare this to the attitudes prevailing in Europe during the sixteenth, seventeenth and eighteenth centuries when both cats and their owners were under constant threat of execution. Historical research by animal behavior expert

Dr. James Serpell of Cambridge University reveals that between 1560 and 1700 many hundreds of innocent and often elderly owners were brutally put to death for no other reason than their friendship with cats. During the trials of the St. Osyth witches at Chelmsford, Essex, in the March of 1582, for example, one Ursula Kemp was charged with having four familiars, or spirits: "Whereof two of them were hes, and the other two were shes: the two he spirits were to punish and kill unto death, and the two shes were to punish with lameness and other diseases of bodily harm." The two he-spirits were Tittey, who appeared in the guise of a gray cat, and Jac, like a black cat.

Another of the accused, one Alice Manfield, was said to have four imps, Robin, Jack, William and Puppet, two hes and two shes "all like unto black cats." Such meager testimony was usually sufficient to condemn the terrified old woman to an agonizing death at the stake, often in the company of the equally unfortunate pets.

But it was a desire for rebellion rather than the fear of sorcery which led eighteenth-century French apprentices to take part in the hideous torture and massacre of innocent cats in a mood of great jollity and high good humor. The historian Robert Darnton explains that these pets were chosen for their symbolic value in a protest against wages and working conditions. To the mob they represented both magic and sexuality. By killing his mistress's well-loved cat, says Darnton, the apprentice was offering both a sexual insult and implying that she was a witch.

Equally ambivalent views may still be found today, although seldom expressed in such cruel terms. My research files are overflowing with letters, interviews, press cuttings and eyewitness accounts all confirming that where cats are concerned, intense feelings are aroused. A recent survey I conducted, based on cruelty reports in national and local newspapers, indicated that in four out of five cases involving the sadistic mistreatment of animals, the victim was a cat or kitten.

Equally, of course, there are hundreds of tales testifying to the deep bonds of affection which can be formed between man and this most independent of pets. Take, for example, the touching story of long-distance truck driver Walter Saul and the kitten he named IMM—International Motorway Moggie!

They first met in the unlovely surroundings of an Istanbul parking lot where Walter had left his truck for the night. As he was climbing into the cab at the start of his long drive home, Walter's attention was attracted by shrieks of feline terror coming from a nearby woodpile. Hurrying across, he discovered two snarling dogs lunging at a terrified tortoiseshell kitten which had taken precarious refuge in a crack between the stacked timbers. With great difficulty, and at considerable risk to himself, Walter succeeded in driving away the snarling dogs. His next task was patiently to coax the terrified creature from its sanctuary. At long last he succeeded in extracting him and carried him to the truck. The kitten was shivering, filthy, bedraggled and half-starved. Yet holding him in his hands, and feeling the little heart racing fearfully beneath his gentle fingers, Walter later explained how he had experienced "an overwhelming desire to make myself responsible for his well-being." It was a decision he never came to regret, despite the expense and inconvenience it caused him. His first task was to calm the kitten down and persuade him to eat. That proved a challenge in itself, since the kitten was too young to lick milk from a saucer and had to be fed from a syringe. But, under Walter's tender, careful nursing, International Motorway Moggie quickly regained his health and strength. As the truck sped along the highways of Europe, IMM was gradually encouraged to try a more substantial diet consisting of chopped chicken and mashed fish.

Far from being frightened by the strange surroundings of the cab, IMM quickly adapted to life on the road and liked nothing better than to snuggle down on Walter's lap as his truck carried them toward the Belgian coast and the boat home.

Well aware of the strict regulations surrounding the importation of animals into England, and having absolutely no intention of trying to smuggle the kitten into the country, Walter's first task, after parking his truck on the cross-Channel ferry, was to report IMM's presence aboard. He was perfectly willing to spend around $1,000 of his own money to keep the kitten in quarantine for the statutory six-month period.

What he was not prepared for was the reception awaiting them in England. Officials curtly informed him that IMM could only be brought into the country provided he produced the necessary import documents. Any attempt to avoid the regulations would lead to Walter's arrest, a fine of £1,000 (around $2,000) and IMM's destruction.

Walter phoned his employer and asked for leave so that he could take IMM back to Belgium, where the kitten could be quarantined while the demands of red tape were satisfied. Not only did his employer immediately give him the time needed, but even offered to pay his return fare. So, within an hour of setting foot on English soil for the first time in weeks, Walter found himself heading back to Belgium instead of home to his family.

Once in Belgium, the pair's luck changed after a sympathetic official and his wife offered to give IMM a home until the import papers arrived. But by the time that happened, the family had grown so fond of IMM, now a sleek and beautiful cat, that they begged Walter to be allowed to keep him. A mutually satisfactory compromise was eventually reached. IMM stayed in Belgium but Walter got "visiting rights" to call in on his old friend whenever his travels took him through the port. This he does regularly, never forgetting to pack a container of IMM's favorite chicken when he calls.

"IMM's a mate," he explained quietly, "and you don't let your mates down."

Walter Saul's behavior and the Belgian official's reaction to IMM's plight are typical of the devotion cats sometimes inspire in people. But what is it about cats which arouses such extremes of love and hate?

Part of the answer to this complex question can be found in those strange and mysterious powers which this book is all about. But it also involves the personality of those who are emotionally attracted by cats and the ways in which these animals are able to satisfy deep psychological needs.

Cat People vs Dog People

You often hear pet owners refer to themselves as "cat" or "dog" lovers and talk about some of the qualities both they and their pets have in common.

Sigmund Freud, the father of psychoanalysis, believed that a desire for close identification with certain animals is deeply rooted in the human unconscious. He called this need "totemism" and pointed out that, in some societies, it takes the form of religious worship. He suggested that when people practice totemism they are trying to acquire some of the mental or physical attributes which the animal in question is believed to possess.

Tribal divisions may form around different totem animals and great antagonism may develop between the opposing groups. Among modern societies, totemism can be seen in the Chinese martial art of Kung Fu, the movements of most of its diverse schools being based on various animals: the cat for cunning, the tiger for speed and ferocity, the monkey for deception, the praying mantis for perseverence, the snake for speed, and so on. Practitioners of these different combat styles strive to imitate both the movements and temperament of their totem animal.

The view that totemism, far from being an outmoded superstition from our distant past, still exerts a powerful force on society is supported by psychological research which has revealed intriguing personality differences between cat- and dog-owners.

Two California-based investigators, Drs. Aline and Robert Kidd, tested the personalities of two hundred men and women whose ages ranged from eighteen to seventy-six. They also collected information about their subjects' preferences for pets. When the results were analyzed, it was clear that dog-lovers differ in important ways from people who would rather own a cat. While 48 percent of dog-owners said that they liked young children, only 30 percent of cat-owners did so. When questioned about their feelings towards adolescents, 30 percent of dog-owners said they enjoyed their company, compared with less than 15 percent of people with cats.

Men who kept cats scored more highly on the trait of "autonomy," indicating that they are more independent and self-sufficient than dog-owners of either sex.

Both male and female cat-fanciers obtained lower scores than people owning dogs on the personality attribute of "nurturance," the desire to involve oneself with other people's lives and problems.

Dog-owning males scored high on "aggression," while women with cats were significantly lower than average on this trait, which suggests that men with dogs are likely to express their wishes and intentions forcefully while women who keep cats will adopt exactly the opposite approach.

Female cat-owners also scored well below average on the trait of "dominance," which means they are less likely to speak up for themselves or to take charge in business or professional relationships.

The portrait of a cat person painted by these research findings is, therefore, very different from that of the typical dog-owner. People who favor cats are more likely to be independent, freedom-loving individuals, self-reliant and slightly aloof from the rest of humanity, preferring not to involve themselves too deeply in the lives of their fellows. They would sooner make their own way in the world, unfettered by the restrictions which society seeks to impose, and avoid confrontations whenever possible through the use of cunning and stealth. When faced with hostility or aggression, they are most likely to retreat into passive resistance, biding their time until the right moment for a clever counterattack.

Dog-owners, on the other hand, tend to be more dependent on others and want to involve themselves in the lives and problems of those around them. They are more likely to be assertive and to confront problems head-on, standing their ground and fighting when challenged. In most situations they feel the need to dominate others and react strongly to any attempts to ride roughshod over their rights.

Notice how strikingly the main features of the cat-owner's personality resemble those of the cat itself. As the great animal expert Konrad Lorenz once said: "The cat is not a socially living animal . . . it is not my prisoner, but an independent being of almost equal status who happens to live in the same house that I do."

Rudyard Kipling expressed this desire for an unrestrained independence and self-sufficiency perfectly when he wrote in his *Just So Stories*: "The wildest of all the wild animals was the Cat. He walked by himself, and all places were alike to him."

People who love cats, therefore, appear to identify with them to such an extent that they gradually absorb this creature's unique traits of temperament into their own personality and outlook on life. If this strikes you as improbable, just consider how swiftly and uncharacteristically aggressive many cat-lovers become whenever their favorite is criticized or attacked. Notice too the desire of many cat-owners to decorate their homes with pictures and posters displaying the cat in all its moods and activities. When I conducted an informal survey of illustrations and models of either cats or dogs in the homes of owners, I discovered that people who keep cats are three times more likely to own such decorations than dog-owners. And a survey of London poster stores confirmed that view, since on average the stores had four pictures depicting cats or kittens for each one illustrating a puppy or dog.

Cat worshippers in preliterate societies showed almost identical attitudes toward the objects of their reverence. Pictures and models were kept around the home and the sacred animal was vigorously defended whenever and however attacked.

Perhaps an echo of those ancient emotions reverberated around the staid surroundings of a British court in 1984 when a jury was asked to pass judgement on rival claims of ownership to a large ginger tom named either Marmaduke Gingerbits or Sunny, depending on whose story was believed.

The defendant, fifty-seven-year-old Monty Cohen, was charged with stealing the cat and assaulting his neighbor, a police officer named John Sewell. Police Constable Sewell explained that when he and his wife had returned from vacation the previous year, they learned that their cat, Marmaduke Gingerbits, was missing from the home of the friend who was taking care of him. Meanwhile, according to the prosecution, a large, well-fed ginger cat had begun visiting another neighbor, Doreen Smythe. She claimed to have seen Monty Cohen trying to catch the cat, which, he said, looked like his missing pet, Sunny.

"The cat wouldn't go near him," recalled Doreen Smythe. "He crouched and was spitting and laid on the floor all hunched up."

Later she saw an advertisement in a shop window which displayed Marmaduke's photograph and offered a £10 reward. PC Sewell went to see Monty Cohen and was shown the animal.

"The cat immediately turned his head and we knew at that moment that it was our animal. He was struggling to get free and get away from Cohen toward myself and my wife."

The case was not resolved on the first hearing, but at a second hearing in June, after a nine-month legal wrangle, it was decided that the cat was indeed Marmaduke Gingerbits. The fact that the case ever came to court well illustrates the passions which cats can arouse in the most law-abiding of citizens.

The Cat's Strengths and Weaknesses

Sight

The physical powers of cats tend to be surrounded by much misunderstanding and confusion. Some people are convinced, for example, that they are able to see extremely well in the dark. This mistaken belief is so widely held that it helped to keep a vital aviation secret during the Second World War. Early in 1941 the RAF's night-fighters began to enjoy increasing success thanks to the introduction of airborne radar. In an attempt to prevent the Germans from realizing the tactical importance of this invention, British propaganda stressed the value of carrots and vitamin A in providing their pilots with night vision as acute as any cat's. Their trump card was fighter ace John Cunningham, whose record number of kills earned him the nickname "Cat's Eyes."

Actually cats have no better vision at night than we do and are farsighted into the bargain, a fact you can easily demonstrate by persuading your cat to play with any small object. When he is engrossed in the game, push the plaything within a couple of inches of his face and you'll see immediate confusion as the object suddenly becomes invisible. Before the game can begin again, he will have to back off until the toy is around six to eight inches away.

Over long distances, however, the cat's eyesight is extremely good, with an effective range of around 120 feet and the ability to detect extremely small movements.

Hearing

Despite their excellent daylight vision, cats rely on ears more than eyes when out hunting, and possess one of the most acute senses of hearing in the animal kingdom. Studies have shown that a cat can recognize its owner's footsteps at a distance of several hundred feet, and almost every owner knows the sudden look of eager anticipation when they detect the click of a distant fridge door or catch the faint sound of a can being opened.

You can see this response to discover just how good your

own cat's hearing is by identifying the "feeding sound" which produces an alert response. Now place him, or her, on one side of a closed door and have somebody make that sound from the other side. Notice the reaction and, if it's obvious the noise has been heard, close another door. You'll be astonished at how many barriers the cat's hearing is able to penetrate.

Movements

Cats are, of course, wonderfully supple creatures with extremely graceful movements. So it comes as something of a surprise to discover that their gait resembles that of a camel or giraffe, with both fore and hind legs on the same side of the body moving in unison. This contrasts with a horse or dog, for example, who move diagonal front and rear limbs together.

The cat's reflexes are superfast, as anybody who has watched one twist in mid-flight after taking a tumble can testify. This ability to land on their feet frequently helps to save them from death after falling from great heights.

The current record-holder in this grim league is a Canadian cat named Gros Minou who tumbled twenty stories on May 1, 1973. Quite how it happened nobody is certain, but one moment Gros Minou was playing on a balcony of his owner's apartment at Forest Hill, near Westmount, Quebec, and the next he was hurtling through space. Passersby watched with horror as the animal turned and tumbled in a fall of more than 300 feet. Gros Minou hit the ground with a sickening thump and the onlookers who ran over fully expected to find a limp corpse. But Gros Minou was very much alive, although he had suffered a fractured pelvis. Prompt veterinary assistance took care of that, however, and a couple of months later Gros Minou was fully restored to health.

Killer Instinct

Despite the fact that the British government "employs" more than 100,000 cats to keep official buildings free from rodents, the present-day cat appears to be a less efficient mouser than even his immediate forebears.

The world's most successful mouser was a tabby named Micky, who slaughtered in excess of 22,000 mice during twenty-three years' service with a Lancashire firm. But since Micky died in 1968, the tradition of mousing and ratting seems to have declined sharply. According to many rodent experts, only one cat in seven now bothers even to chase them, which is one reason why the world's rodent population has increased by an alarming 30 percent during the last few years.

This lack of enthusiasm for the chase may be explained in two ways. Firstly, most cats are so well fed that they see no reason to go out and catch their dinner. But even more importantly, the present-day cat is actually much less aggressive than even recent ancestors.

Selective breeding, designed to create the tame, docile, affectionate animal most owners would regard as the perfect pet, has produced a species more interested in stretching out by the fire than sneaking through damp undergrowth in search of prey.

Sensitivity to Temperature

When advertisers want to symbolize luxurious comfort, they often depict a cat curled on a sofa before a blazing fire. It's an image with more than a grain of truth, for cats have an extraordinary sensitivity to tiny changes in the sur-

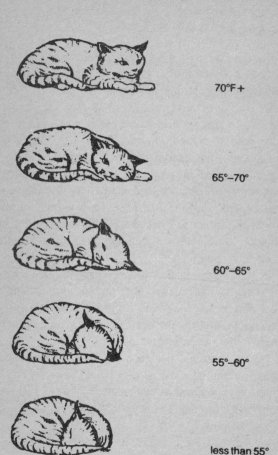

70°F +

65°–70°

60°–65°

55°–60°

less than 55°

How to tell the temperature from your cat's sleeping position.

rounding temperature. In fact, so great is this ability that a German animal expert, Dr. Hans Precht, discovered that it is possible to get an accurate idea of room temperature just by looking at the way a cat sleeps. The chart opposite, based on his study of more than four hundred positions, allows you to use your pet as a living thermometer.

The cat, then, possesses many unique physical qualities, although not always those for which it is famed. But it also possesses a superior IQ and is one of the cleverest creatures you'll ever meet.

CHAPTER 2

Your
Brilliant Cat

I met Eggbag, the magical cat, while in New York to interview researchers studying animal intelligence. Having spent most of the day surrounded by sophisticated laboratory equipment and learned talk in university psychology departments, the last thing I expected to discover was an unusual example of feline brilliance on the dusty sidewalks of the city's far from elegant Eighth Avenue.

It was a blazing hot afternoon in late July and the pavements were crowded with people, many of whom were converging on a store bearing the name The Magic Center. Intrigued, I joined the throng and finally succeeded in squeezing my way into the congested showroom. Which is where I came across Eggbag, a cat whose conjuring skills leave even experienced magicians rubbing their heads in amazement.

The gray-and-white cat performs his tricks to capacity crowds, not before the TV cameras or in front of a music hall audience but on the counter of a store selling magical apparatus to conjurers. According to his owner, magician Russ Delmar, the cat showed considerable conjuring potential while still a kitten, and so earned himself the name Eggbag, after a piece of magical equipment. Russ attracts afternoon shoppers with a variety of sleight-of-hand tricks, making coins, billiard balls and cards appear and disappear with practiced ease. But both he and his audience know that the true star of the impromptu shows, and the performer who pulls the crowds, is Eggbag.

The afternoon I was there, the cat slept peacefully throughout his master's tricks. Eventually, however, he opened an eye and surveyed the crowd thoughtfully as though making up his mind whether it was sufficiently large and enthusiastic to be worthy of his talents. Deciding that he would perform, Eggbag rose slowly and, after a long and languid stretch, strolled down the counter to Russ's side. A murmur of delighted anticipation came from the audience as his master immediately shuffled, fanned and held out a pack of cards, inviting the nearest bystander to take one: "But don't let the cat see it," he warned.

A card was chosen and replaced in the pack, which Russ deftly reshuffled. Fanning the cards again, he held them out to Eggbag. Without a moment's hesitation the cat pounced, catching a card in his mouth and pulling it free from the pack.

"What card did you select?" Russ asked.

"Four of hearts," the customer replied.

With a grin, Russ extracted the card from Eggbag's mouth and placed it face up on the counter. It was the four of hearts.

"The first time I saw this trick I damn nearly fell through the floor," one of the regulars told me. "I still can't figure out exactly how it's done."

But while the star of this Eighth Avenue store is clearly a skilled performer with considerable charisma, Eggbag is far from unusual in being a very smart cat.

The fact is that most cats are extremely bright, possessing an IQ which is, in many ways, far superior to that of dogs and surpassed in the animal kingdom only by man's closest relatives, monkeys and chimps. If you're a cat owner, this news may not come as much of a surprise, because these clever creatures often impress those who care for them with their powerful intellects. Even so, it is unlikely that you are fully aware of your pet's true intellectual potential, for cats are able to display levels of intelligence that astonish scientists and make the fortunes of businessmen astute enough to capitalize on their cleverness.

One of the first to do so was Pietro Capelli, a poorly educated nineteenth-century Italian showman who gained an international reputation and considerable wealth from his troupe of performing cats. Capelli, using secret training methods which died with him, taught these animals tricks of such amazing complexity and skill that they were invited to perform in all the courts of Europe. Even when one allows for the likely exaggeration of contemporary accounts, Capelli's shows must have been truly sensational. Cats swung from trapezes, balanced on high wires, rode in carts, and even lay on their backs to juggle with their hind legs. They sharpened knives using a paw-powered grinding wheel, prepared rice Italian style using a mortar and pestle, played on children's musical instruments and drew water from a model well, supplying exactly the number of buckets their master had asked for. Throughout the whole performance Capelli stood on the sidelines, hardly giving a single command, although when he did, it could come in any of the three languages in which both he and his cats were fluent.

As a child in Tuscany, Capelli had shown a deep love of cats, despite having been born in a city slum to a family far too poor to enjoy the luxury of keeping a pet. While other boys played in the back alleys, young Pietro would visit the municipal garbage dumps and overgrown waste-land where cats lived wild and survived by their wits.

All he learned about cats came not from books but through firsthand observation, by squatting for hours amidst piles of rubbish or crouching painfully behind the cover of bushes, watching the animals at work and play. In this way he gained the deep, practical insights which would, one day, help him to enjoy fame and fortune. Ca-pelli not only observed cats, he helped them to survive, tending the injured, nursing the sick and scrounging food, often going hungry himself, so that his friends could have enough to eat.

One day, partly to amuse himself and partly to discover how easy it would be to train them, Capelli started teaching his cats some simple tricks. To his surprise and delight they not only learned their lessons quickly and well, but really appeared to enjoy performing them. Before long he had taught his small troupe a large number of tricks and was putting on shows for the local children. News of Capelli's shows spread rapidly around the neighborhood and started attracting crowds of adults as well as youngsters. Within just a few months, and without advertising his troupe in any way, Capelli and his cats were performing regularly before large and enthusiastic audiences. Capelli's Cats, which in their day were an act as popular as any present-day pop group, had made it to the top.

Japan has produced a modern version of Capelli in thirty-two-year-old Satoru Tsuda, who heads one of the country's top poster agencies. A few years ago Tsuda hit on the idea that trained cats would be a big attraction in television commercials. He appealed for strays and received more than 700 offers. Some people wrote or phoned, but many others simply dumped their unwanted pets outside his front door. From these hopefuls, Tsuda selected four especially photogenic animals to be groomed for stardom. He then devoted a great deal of his time to their training, annoying some of his colleagues, who were still extremely skeptical about the whole project. He taught his cats to perform a number of tricks, including standing on their hind legs, assuming and holding poses for the camera and—most difficult of all—wearing an extensive wardrobe of costumes, especially created for the cats at a cost of $564 each.

But Tsuda's hard work swiftly paid handsome dividends. The cats were an instant hit with advertisers and soon began appearing on TV commercials, in magazine advertisements and on billboards all over Japan. They quickly became so popular that manufacturers fought for the expensive privilege of reproducing their pictures on calendars, diaries, pendants, brooches and posters.

The cats posed as street toughs, clad in black leather jackets, sporting Samurai warrior headbands and standing beside miniature motorbikes; they were photographed as a rock band complete with punk costumes and electric guitars; as schoolgirls, teachers, policemen, soldiers, and housewives whisking a broom across a perfect model of a middle-class Japanese home.

The posing skills of Tsuda's cats turned them into a media sensation, creating a craze which is still sweeping the nation. With their pictures on more than 500 products, and their commercials drawing audiences as large as most TV programs, the cats are reputed to be earning their owner well over $1 million a month.

But Tsuda takes good care of the animals. Strays who once scavenged among garbage cans for their suppers today enjoy a life of luxury, eating the finest food money can buy, living in warm, comfortable, elegant and secure surroundings, cared for by a full-time staff and having their health supervised, around the clock, by Japan's leading vets.

On its own, of course, an ability to learn new tricks quickly and perform them successfully need not indicate any great mental ability. Given sufficient time, patience and the right kinds of skills, it is possible to train virtually any animal, as American psychologist Dr. Leon Smith has demonstrated.

Using his own specially developed training procedures, called Behavioral Engineering Technique (BET), Dr. Smith has persuaded all manner of unlikely creatures to perform tasks previously considered impossible by most animal experts. He has taught brown bears to enjoy a game of basketball and is the proud owner of the world's only performing fish, three golden carp who can ring a bell on command, smoke cigarettes and pick the queen from a pack of playing cards.

Dr. Smith obtains his remarkable results using a well-established procedure known as "operant conditioning." To understand what this powerful procedure is and why it allows even unintelligent creatures like carp to learn such complicated tricks, we must take a trip back in time, to the turn of this century and the St. Petersburg laboratory of a Russian physiologist, Professor Ivan Petrovich Pavlov.

Pavlov's research interest was in discovering the workings of the digestive system. To do this he carried out numerous experiments with dogs, one of which was to measure how much saliva they produced immediately prior to eating. This study led to an unexpected but extremely important observation. When an assistant brought the dogs food, they produced more saliva in anticipation of a meal.

That was hardly surprising, but then Pavlov noticed that, after a while, the dogs increased their production of saliva not when they saw the meat but when they heard the assistant's footsteps in the passage outside. Later he demonstrated that the dogs could be trained to increase their output of saliva in the presence of any sort of stimulus, a bell ringing for example, provided that it was originally produced in the presence of food. Pavlov called this response a conditioned reflex, and the process by which it was obtained became known as classical conditioning.

Pavlov's discoveries fascinated many psychologists and helped the American researcher John Broadus Watson from 1913 onward to develop an extremely influential branch of psychology called behaviorism. Later Watson's ideas were elaborated by another U.S. psychologist, the Harvard-based Burrhus Frederic Skinner, in the 1930s.

The behaviorists believed that all behavior, human and animal, could be explained on the basis of conditioned reflexes. Some, they argued, arose in exactly the same way that Pavlov's dogs learned to produce saliva at the sound of a bell. Others arose through a process which Skinner termed "operant conditioning." By this he meant that an animal, or human, was more likely to continue with some activity if it produced a reward. While this might sound like little more than common sense, its implications were profound in that they seemed to many to provide a complete explanation for each and every kind of behavior. Learning, they argued, was a process depending on two key concepts, "shaping" and "reinforcement."

Using only these two procedures, which form the basis of Dr. Leon Smith's Behavioral Engineering Technique, it is possible, at least in theory, to teach any animal to perform any task of which it is physically capable.

To illustrate how learning theory worked in practice,

Professor Skinner sometimes demonstrated the potency of shaping and reinforcement by training pigeons to play table tennis, using miniature rackets, during the course of a lecture. While speaking, Skinner would keep a watchful eye on the birds. When one moved toward a racket, he would immediately give it a food pellet. Next it had to touch the racket with its beak to get a pellet, then actually pick up the racket to receive any food. This process continued until the pigeons finally ended up playing Ping-Pong.

You could, if you wished, use similar procedures to train your cat in a vast repertoire of tasks. Suppose, for instance, you wanted your cat to fetch your slippers when you sat down by the fire. Your first task would be to observe him very carefully and offer a reward (the reinforcement), such as a tasty tidbit, any time he went anywhere near the slippers. The cat would quickly realize that an easy way to get a snack was to hang around your slippers. At that point you would stop rewarding him for going near your slippers and only offer the reinforcement when he touched them.

Now comes the trickiest part of all—persuading the cat to pick up one of the slippers. Although some animals will spontaneously try to lift a slipper in their mouths (after a tidbit has been hidden beneath it, at which point you immediately reward that action), others are much more reluctant to do so. These animals can often be coaxed into lifting and carrying a slipper by taking a small piece of ribbon and attaching it in the form of a loop to the cat's favorite toy—something light and easy to pick up in the mouth. The cat is then encouraged to take this in his mouth, by actually placing the loop of ribbon gently between the jaws and rewarding him for holding it there, however briefly. In time, the cat will accept the loop and begin to enjoy lifting up the toy in order to receive a tasty snack.

Slowly but surely you encourage your pet to transport

the toy across the room. When this task has been perfected, remove the toy and exchange it for a piece of cardboard cut into the shape of a slipper. At first the cat may be puzzled by the unfamiliar object, but will soon learn to play the new game. At this point you are ready to transfer the ribbon loop to a pair of light slippers. The cat, having grown used to carrying things around and bringing them to you by means of the loop of ribbon, should quickly master this final skill and fetch your slippers as efficiently as any well-trained dog.

But, clearly, true intelligence involves much more than responding in such a mechanical manner to a set of pre-determined signals. It demands a capacity for abstract thinking and reasoning, the ability to plan logically and think creatively when confronted by novel challenges and unfamiliar problems. Only if cats are capable of performing mentally demanding tasks of this nature can they really be considered intelligent. Evidence from laboratory experiments strongly suggests that they do, in fact, possess these high-level intellectual skills.

At Wesleyan University, Dr. Donald Adams has shown that cats can remember succcessful problem-solving strategies and employ insight to think their way out of unusual situations.

In one series of experiments, he placed cats inside small boxes from which escape was difficult but not impossible. Sometimes lifting the lid involved discovering and operating a hidden catch. On other occasions the task was far harder. For example, the cat might have to stretch a paw through a hole in the box and pull down a string.

When first placed in the box, all the cats tried to escape by means of brute force, pushing against the sides or scratching furiously at the lid. But this approach was quickly abandoned when it proved unsuccessful and the animals began to investigate various cunning escape strategies. What especially impressed Dr. Adams was that, almost from the start, the cats behaved intelligently, trying one method after another until one worked and they could climb out.

As soon as they had escaped, Dr. Adams replaced them in the box and observed their behavior carefully. He wanted to find out whether they repeated the same trial-and-error approach adopted the first time or escaped much more rapidly by employing the same successful solution. If they did this, then the cats were not responding unthinkingly but were showing a considerable understanding of both the problem and its solution.

After analyzing the results, Dr. Adams was left in no doubt that his cats had been using thinking of a high order. They did understand how they had escaped and remembered exactly what needed to be done to solve the problem. In that moment of inspiration when they realized how to escape from the box, Dr. Adams's cats seem to have enjoyed what we sometimes call a "Eureka" experience. It's the moment when the veil of confusion falls from one's eyes and the answer becomes blindingly obvious. Donald Adams provides a graphic description of how such a flash of insight came to one of his other cats, named Tom, who was called on to solve the tricky problem of getting his paws on a tempting slice of liver tied to the end of a long piece of string. The snag was that the liver hung inside a wire cage and Tom was on the outside. Dr. Adams recalls:

> Tom walked all round the cage and looked over the whole situation from all sides, but did not once paw through the sides toward the liver. He frequently looked up at the string to the place where it was tied, sometimes staring intently at it for some seconds.

Finally, after one of these pauses, when he had been in the situation a total of two minutes and thirty seconds, he turned away suddenly from his intent stare, went to the right back corner and climbed to the top of the cage. He went directly to the center, reached through the top and pawed up a loop of the string but was unable to bring this through the wire.

Dr. Adams made the cat's task slightly easier by untying the string and fastening it to a small stick which he then put on the roof of the cage. When Tom was allowed back to the cage he immediately climbed to the top and clawed at the string where it was knotted to the stick. Then, watched carefully by Dr. Adams and his colleagues, Tom grasped the string in his teeth, moved several inches backwards and sat down. With a sweeping motion of his right foreleg, he caught the string and raised the liver about a foot. Standing on the loose string to prevent the liver dropping down again, Tom took the string in his mouth. Then he jumped lightly to the floor, the string clasped between his teeth, confident that the slice of liver would follow.

As a result of his research, Dr. Adams concluded that cats possess almost the same high level of problem-solving ability skills as is found in monkeys, previously considered to be the only animals, apart from man, who could use insight to answer problems. To test this belief he devised a task which could be performed with equal physical ease by both cats and monkeys, that is one in which the greater manipulative ability of the monkey's hand and the animal's superior strength could not confer any advantage.

Instead of boxes with hidden catches, Adams trained his cats to pull a box on wheels around the laboratory. When they were used to doing this, he suspended a piece of liver on a long string from the ceiling and positioned one of the boxes some two feet away. Then he turned loose a female tabby called Tabs.

The cat immediately climbed onto the box and stretched repeatedly toward the liver. Next she got down from the box and stood beneath the meat, attempting, without any success, to catch it with her paw. Realizing that this method wasn't going to succeed, Tabs went away to think things over. She sat down in a corner of the laboratory and began grooming herself without giving the tidbit a second glance.

Donald Adams describes what happens next: "She suddenly paused and became rigid for a period of four or five seconds, in the posture of washing, with one hind leg sticking up . . ." Tabs was now staring intently at the liver, her ears pricked forward and body tense. Rising abruptly, she ran to the box and pulled it across the floor until it stood directly beneath the meat. Then she jumped lightly onto the box, grabbed the liver and settled down to enjoy a well-deserved snack.

Discussing Dr. Adams's findings, the eminent animal psychologist V. Krechevsky comments: "The learning process *at every point* consisted of a series of integrated, purposive behavior patterns."

Tom and Tabs were not behaving in the automatic, unthinking way associated with operant conditioning, shaping and reinforcement but were working toward their goal of gaining the liver in a reasoned and intelligent manner.

When monkeys were given exactly the same task, they found the solution slightly—but only slightly—more quickly.

Both animals revealed much greater problem-solving skills than dogs who, after managing to escape from the boxes for the first time, continued to use trial-and-error methods on subsequent occasions. It took them far longer to realize that a strategy which had worked successfully on one occasion could usefully be tried again in similar situations.

A different type of intellectual skill was demanded in experiments described by V. Dethier, Professor of Biology at Princeton University, and Eliot Stellar, Professor of Physiological Psychology at the University of Pennsylvania. Here the intelligence-assessing task involved a device known as the "triple plate problem," in which the animal must learn to press the plates in a predetermined order. The purpose of this test is to investigate the cat's ability to learn and recall complex patterns. Each session usually starts with a very short, simple sequence and builds gradually to long and complicated combinations. When the plates are pressed in the correct sequence, the animal is rewarded with food. The study showed that even small kittens are experts when it comes to solving extremely complicated "triple plate" sequences, managing to recall correctly combinations involving up to seven separate presses. This performance outclasses all other animals except monkeys, who can master up to twenty press sequences.

The IQs of cats and dogs were compared directly in a series of experiments described by Drs. N. Maier, Professor of Psychology at the University of Michigan, and T. Schneirla, Curator at the Department of Animal Behavior at the American Museum of Natural History. Their animals were shown a large number of boxes and taught that food could only be found under the one which had a lighted lamp on top. Once the training was completed, the identification light was turned on only briefly and the animal prevented, for varying amounts of time, from approaching any of the boxes. The idea was to discover how long it would be able to remember which box contained the reward. The researchers discovered that, while dogs are only capable of remembering this information for up to five minutes, cats went to the correct box as long as sixteen hours later, a recall superior to even monkeys and orangutans.

These results did more than confirm that cats have excellent memories, however, since to retain information both about the importance of the lamp and the fact that it was associated with the food box meant that the cats must have formed some complex, abstract concept in their brains— one of the key elements of real intellectual ability.

Cats differ intellectually from any other species, including dogs, in other important ways too, as research psychologist Dr. H. Szymanski has shown. After making detailed comparisons among many different species, he concluded that animals can be placed in one of two major categories. Some, like dogs, rely mainly on the senses of touch and smell when exploring their surroundings. Cats, on the other hand, place far more emphasis on sights and sounds. In performing a variety of intellectually demanding tasks they usually emerge as clear winners.

In one experiment, scientists decided to see how efficient cats, dogs and chickens were when it came to locating a hidden sound source. They set up a number of screens and placed a loudspeaker behind one of them. The speaker was connected to a tape recorder which produced sounds of specific interest to the animal being tested; for example the chicken could hear the clucking of chicks, while the cat heard a mouse squeaking. Whenever the animal approached the correct screen, it was rewarded with food. Gradually the screens were moved closer and closer to each other in order to discover which animal could make the finest discrimination. The chicken did worst on this test, followed by the dog. The cat was the outright winner.

Not only are cats sensitive to the slightest sounds, and extremely good at locating the source of particular noises, but they also have a very wide auditory range, being able to detect tones of up to 50,000 cycles per second, which far exceeds human hearing with its upper limit of around 18,000 cycles per second.

In experiments which demonstrate both the learning skills of cats and yet another aspect of their superb hearing, Dr. Richard Zeliony has shown that they can also make fine discriminations between musical tones. By rewarding his cats for each correct response, Dr. Zeliony quickly trained them to run in from a nearby room whenever he blew a whistle pitched at middle C. Before long the cats had learned to distinguish middle C from whistles as close in pitch as one half tone, for which they received no reward. This meant that his cats came along eagerly whenever they heard middle C but completely ignored a whistle in, for example, C sharp. This is an accomplishment which many humans would be unable to equal, and it also sets cats apart from other members of the animal kingdom in that most species are tone deaf.

Many of the animal experts I met, both in Europe and the United States, are certain that cats' superior capabilities could prove of tremendous practical benefit to mankind.

Dr. Leon Smith, inventor of the BET training method, believes cats could be taught to do almost any type of work, from operating factory assembly lines and controlling machinery to household chores. Furthermore, he is convinced that they would be a great deal happier in handling these humdrum tasks than the humans they replaced. His view is shared by André Marcal, a leading French animal researcher, who has explored ways in which a vast range of equipment might be modified so that animals could operate it.

American specialist Arnold Aronson believes that, within the next five years, our knowledge of the brain's neurotransmitters—the substances which transmit information in the nervous system—will be sufficient to increase the intellectual capacity of many life forms, including humans. He also feels that a combination of sophisticated training techniques, like BET, and drugs could result in a new breed of supercats, capable of performing a wide range of complex skills. André Marcal, who has spent years investigating the tasks these cats might accomplish, thinks it would be fairly easy to train them to obey such instructions as: "Take this message to the office manager" or: "Go to the supermarket with my shopping list."

Engineers and designers have assured me it would be relatively simple either to modify many items of existing household, office and factory equipment for cat control, or to construct new tools custom built to be operated by animals. In many cases all that would be needed is the fitting of a switch large enough to be pressed by a paw or nose. With such a gadget, which anyone with a small amount of mechanical skill and electrical knowledge could construct quickly and cheaply, cats could easily be taught to switch on the TV, radio or hi-fi, control the central heating (remember how sensitive the cat is to temperature changes), open the door for you—but not to a stranger—switch on the oven to start supper cooking so that it was ready when you returned home, sound an alarm if an intruder comes anywhere near your house (their keen hearing would be invaluable here), trigger a fire alarm at the first whiff of smoke (they have an excellent sense of smell), and switch on the kettle at the right time for your early morning tea.

One group of cat-owners for whom such helpers might provide vital assistance are the disabled, bedridden and paralyzed. Some preliminary work has already been done in this area by training monkeys to assist the physically handicapped. Even fairly small monkeys are capable of performing a number of useful tasks, such as spoon-feeding an invalid, combing their hair, cutting up their food, preparing drinks and even shaving male patients. But a problem with monkeys is that they are temperamental creatures who can suddenly turn vicious. Indeed, the primates as a whole are so unpredictable that some zookeepers regard the larger ones, like chimpanzees or orangutans, as more dangerous to deal with than lions and tigers. Since severely handicapped people would be quite incapable of defending themselves against any such attack, special measures must be taken to safeguard them before doctors sanction the use of monkey helpers. At present the only way this can be done is by the cruel strategy of pulling out all the monkey's teeth.

Animal experts who favor cats for these tasks point out that not only are they a lot cheaper and easier to obtain, but they can be trained just as quickly to perform tasks no less complicated. With modern engineering methods it is perfectly possible to construct mechanical arms and hands that could take over where paws would fail. Unlike dogs, which tend to be clumsy in their movements and require regular walking, cats possess the subtle delicacy of movement necessary for operating electronic equipment. Additional advantages are that the cat needs no walking, is very clean in its habits and has sufficient agility to reach almost any nook and cranny in the patient's home to fetch wanted objects.

With proper training, the cat could not only take care of the immediate physical needs of its owner, but run errands, taking prescriptions to the pharmacy and messages to friends. André Marcal believes that the cat could serve not only as "a home help, but as a bright friend. Loyal, friendly and intelligent, it could prove the ideal companion."

Far from condemning such a free spirit to a life of household drudgery, it seems likely that the cat would love its work. All the research shows that animals enjoy putting their newly acquired skills to work and actually look forward to it.

To perform any of these tasks, of course, it would be helpful if one could communicate with the cat and understand the animal's replies. Fortunately this should prove perfectly possible, since research has shown that cats can hold highly intelligent and revealing conversations with their owners once their subtle and complex language has been learned.

CHAPTER 3

The Hidden Language of Cats

Although Mimi was a beautiful pedigree Chinchilla and Kiki a humble and fairly elderly canary, the two pets enjoyed a remarkably warm friendship in the Paris apartment of their owner, Madame Rainer. The bird, who was allowed to fly freely around the apartment, never showed the slightest fear of the cat, and when they played together, as they frequently did, Mimi was always very careful to be gentle with her friend.

One morning, however, Madame Rainer found the canary dead. Although there wasn't a mark on the canary's body, she felt that Mimi must have got too rough and frightened the little bird to death. In her distress, she shouted angrily at her cat before starting to cry.

Mimi gazed at her mistress's tear-streaked face for a moment and then abruptly left the apartment. She was away nearly thirty-six hours, returning toward dusk the following day with a young, live and completely unharmed bird in her mouth.

What made this obvious peace-offering even more surprising was that the breed of bird Mimi carried home could not have come from either the city itself or even the surrounding suburbs. The only explanation was that the cat had traveled several miles into the country in search of a suitable replacement for the dead canary.

This extraordinary story offers an excellent example of the cat's ability to understand human feelings by interpreting not only the words we use but also the silent signals of body language which accompany them.

But communication between cats and humans does not have to be all one way. By taking a little time and trouble it is possible to gain a good knowledge of the vast repertoire of language which cats regularly employ when communicating with one another and attempting to converse with us.

If you've always believed that a cat's conversation consists of nothing more interesting than a few meows and the occasional purrs, the idea of enjoying a worthwhile chat with one may sound somewhat unlikely. Yet learning cat talk is essential if you want to achieve real insight into their thoughts, desires, intentions and feelings.

Scientists have discovered, for example, that while dogs only employ some forty sounds, cats regularly use over a hundred, and possess one of the largest spoken vocabularies found anywhere in the animal kingdom, including among chimpanzees and gorillas.

But this is only part of the story, since sounds are combined with a large number of body signals, such as facial expressions and tail movements, each conveying important messages about the animal's outlook on life.

In addition, cats produce special chemicals that enable

them to communicate over distances, stake out territory and indicate sexual responsiveness. Other animals use odors for similar purposes, of course, but you may not be too surprised to learn that cats have come up with some subtle differences to give their scent signals greater power.

Exploring Cat Talk

As with humans, cats often have individual ways of expressing themselves, and it would take a whole book to describe all the sounds they can produce, so here I shall only consider the most important and frequently employed features of their extensive vocabulary.

A serious difficulty in writing about cat language is attempting to do justice to the nuances of sound produced in different situations. If you are seriously interested in exploring this subject, the best way is to make your own recordings and compare them with the descriptions given below. You can do this quite easily, using low-cost cassette equipment (and I'll be offering advice about ways of getting the best quality recordings toward the end of this chapter).

But even if you don't want to go to this extra trouble, just by reading my descriptions carefully and then both listening to and observing your own cat in action you will quickly learn to understand much of their language. Since I will also be explaining how to talk back to your cat, you can then use this knowledge to start an enjoyable two-way conversation.

During the past ten years, animal psychologists have devoted thousands of hours to recording, analyzing and interpreting the language of cats. The most detailed of these has been conducted by Dr. Mildren Moelk, an eminent researcher based in Rochester, New York, who has spent many years observing and recording hundreds of cats.

Her work shows that cats produce sounds, as we do, by passing air from the lungs through two fibrous, elastic, vocal cords located in the larynx. Unlike humans, however, a cat does not use the tip of its tongue to give shape to these sounds but, instead, creates thirteen distinct vowels by varying the muscle tension in its mouth, throat, face and lips. The cat also produces seven to eight consonant sounds by closing and shaping its mouth in various ways in order to alter the resonance.

Dr. Moelk has identified three main groups of cat sounds:

- Murmurs—made with the mouth closed.
- Calls—the mouth is open to start with but slowly closes while the sound continues.
- Cries—the mouth remains tense and open throughout.

Humans have to be consistent in the sounds we make, in order to ensure we express ourselves comprehensibly in any particular language. Cats, by comparison, are free to combine vowels and consonants in a far more flexible manner, a fact which allows them to employ a much wider range of sounds in their conversations than we do. Furthermore, whether living in luxury or surviving by their wits, all cats share a similar language and give voice to express themselves in much the same way. So let's explore this language in greater detail, starting with the first of Dr. Moelk's three sound categories.

Murmurs

PURRING

Cats produce this distinctive sound by vibrating two folds of mucous membrane, known as the "false vocal cords," located at the lower end of the voice box.

Cat-owners tend to assume that purring is the obvious sign of a contented cat. While this is usually correct, there may also be occasions on which it is a misleading assumption. Furthermore, this rather general interpretation tends to obscure the shades of sound and meaning that a knowledgeable owner is able to discover in their message.

Listen carefully and you'll soon realize that purring is not one sound but consists of several similar sounds varying in frequency and intensity. By introducing these subtle changes, the cat is able to communicate a wide variety of feelings.

Rough purrs: The "rougher" the purr, that is, the more distinct the sound of each beat, the more intense is the cat's pleasure. It's the feline equivalent of "I love it, I love it, please don't stop . . ."

Smooth purrs: As the cat begins to get bored, or drowsy, the purr grows smoother, making it more difficult to distinguish between the individual beats. The cat is telling you that, while the activity has been enjoyable up to that point, he's now had enough and would sooner stop. It's a way of saying, "That was great. Just what I needed."

Smooth high purrs: A second type of smooth purr is used to signal eager attention and the desire to obtain something which the cat anticipates will bring pleasure.

You can identify this by the addition of a high, healthy, "rrr" sound that seems to come from the chest area. Whenever your cat sends this message, he has spotted something especially desirable—food, a plaything or the possibility of your petting him—and is telling you: "Yes, yes, I must have that . . ."

Distress purrs: Cats don't purr from pleasure alone, but can sometimes make this sound when in extreme pain or if seriously unwell. Why they should use the same signal to convey both enjoyment and great distress remains a mystery but it has, occasionally, misled cat-owners into believing their pet was recovering from an illness, when he was really getting worse. So if your cat starts purring for no apparent reason, after being sick or seeming in pain, it would be sensible to take him along to the vet for a checkup.

MURMURING

Greeting murmurs: This single purr inhalation combines an initial "m" sound with the breathy "rrr" quality of the smooth purr described above, and sounds like "mhrhrhrn." It's a friendly "hello" reserved almost entirely for humans and it may be extended in a series of inhalations as your cat runs to meet you. It may also be produced with a trilled "r," to sound like "mrrr" to register delight at some other kind of greeting, for instance when the cat settles down in his bed.

Calling murmurs: These resemble greeting murmurs in some ways but begin with an "uh" noise, caused by the cat using a *glottal stop* instead of a relaxed mouth, and sound like: "uhmhrhrhrnnn."

A glottal stop is produced by trapping the exhaled air through the rapid closure of the vocal cords. An Englishman with a Cockney accent uses a glottal stop when saying the word "bottle."

The general meaning of this murmur is "come here" but the signal varies in emphasis from a gentle plea to a crisp command, depending on who or what is being summoned.

Acknowledgment murmurs: This quick, short, inhaled purring tone drops rapidly in pitch, ending in a nasal "ng" consonant, to give a "mhhhng" sound. It is often made when a cat is given, or realizes he is about to receive, some hoped-for tidbit or toy. It may be directed toward you or another cat and is as close as cats ever come to saying "thanks."

The coaxing murmur: Produced in response to something the cat desires, it consists of a "mrrrraahou," with the "r" being trilled, and can best be translated as: "Please do what I want . . ."

Calls

Calls are produced while the mouth slowly closes, as in the familiar "meow." When giving voice to the "aou" part of this call, the "a" is made with the jaws open, while the "o" and "u" are created by gradually closing the mouth. Here are the five most frequently heard calls.

THE DEMAND

This consists of two sounds, the first similar to the inhaled, coaxing "mhrhrn" described above, the second being made up of an exhaled, extended cluster of vowels. Together they produce a "mhrhrnaaaahou" with the "aaah" element lengthened and stressed. As the demand becomes more insistent, the "aaah" is given even greater emphasis while the "r" gradually changes to an "i" sound, ending up as an extended "meow."

If a cat fails to have his needs satisfied or expectations met, he frequently protests at this disappointment by relaxing the stress on the "aaaah," while putting emphasis on, and lengthening, the "o" and "u" portions of the call. This changes the utterance, to a weaker, more hopeless and more bewildered sounding version of the original.

THE BEGGING DEMAND

A modification of the demand call, this cry extends the "o" and "u" sounds to produce a 'mhrhrhrnnaaaahooouuu," which is more prolonged than the straight demand because the mouth closes more slowly. The cat uses this call when all his attention is focused on some especially sought-after goal, such as a tidbit or favorite toy. It's the equivalent of: "Please, please, please let me have it!"

THE BEWILDERMENT CALL

When the initial "aah" of any of the cat's repertoire of "meows" is louder and more drawn out than the remainder of the cry, it's a clear indication that the animal is both excited about something and confident that his expectations will be met. The outcome of some activity, such as your preparing a snack for him, is being taken for granted. If anything happens to prevent that goal from being realized— perhaps you are called away to the phone before setting the dish down—he is very likely to signal his unhappiness and frustration by ending his call on a prolonged "u" sound made with a rising inflection. This causes the "u" to dominate even though it is not given any special emphasis. The best translation of the resulting "maahouuuu" is: "Hey, what on earth is happening?"

THE WORRIED CALL

When your cat feels anxious or worried over the failure to obtain a desired goal, he modifies the bewilderment call by cutting short the previously drawn out "aah" so that it sounds rather like the "a" in "cat." This produces a "maaouuuu" sound which is usually combined with several of the body language signals expressing concern that I shall be describing in a moment.

THE COMPLAINING CALL

This sounds like "mhhngaahou" with the "ng" being produced by a glottal stop. It is a cry which varies considerably according to the kind of emotion your cat intends to express. When the "aah" part is drawn out, the call becomes a scolding message, your cat is cross with you—or another cat—over some infringement of his rights and is expressing this irritation in no uncertain terms. It is the human equivalent of "How could you do this to me!"

When the emphasis is on the final "u," on the other hand, your cat is expressing a weak and rather dejected complaint, much as if a human told you sadly: "And I always thought you liked me!" If you hear this cry, be sure to reassure your cat by speaking sympathetically and giving him some extra petting.

Cries

The final group of sounds to consider are cries produced with the mouth open and jaw, facial and vocal muscles tensed. These are the familiar and unpleasant "caterwaulings" heard when cats are fighting, threatening each other or mating.

THE REFUSAL CRY

This is a low-pitched, disjointed, raspy cry containing an "oe" vowel sound which has no close equivalent in English but is heard in *"oeuf,"* the French word for egg.

It sounds like "oe-oe-oe-oe," where the dashes indicate a wavering note, and the overall effect is similar to that produced by the ignition of a car whose battery is flat. It is a protest voiced when the cat is being forced to do something he finds objectionable and is preparing to resist vigorously. A rather threatening message, its human equivalent is "Lay off or else!"

You may well hear such a cry the first time you attempt to put a collar on your cat.

SPITTING

Cats make a variety of spitting noises. One quick, short "pffft" cry produced by the release of a burst of air through closed lips is a completely involuntary sound made when startled or frightened. Its closest human equivalent would be the startled "aaaaagh" that escapes your lips when something nasty happens without warning.

But there is also the completely voluntary and rather more familiar "chchchchchchchchch" cry directed toward any strange cats who have had the temerity to trespass on his territory. This resembles the ''ch'' sound in the word ''loch'' and is usually accompanied by flattened ears, narrowed eyes and bared canine teeth, silent signals for aggression. The message here is exactly the same as that being sent out by an angry bull as he menacingly paws the ground. Contrary to popular belief, neither indicates an immediate attack. Indeed the whole purpose of these ritualized aggression signals is to prevent conflict by deterring the other animal.

THE ANGER WAIL

You'll hear this cry whenever two cats are in dispute over some piece of territory.

Starting with the mouth open, it consists of a long drawn out sound produced by slowly opening and closing the mouth. This results in a long ''wwwaaaaaahoooouuwww'' with the canine teeth prominently displayed, the head slightly tilted, and gaze firmly fixed on the intruder. With both cats in full cry one is reminded of nothing less than a class of saber-toothed tigers in the prehistoric jungles.

If you hear this wail you'll know your affectionate pet has been momentarily transformed into a savage predator completely in the grip of an evolutionary imperative to protect his territory at almost any price. If you intervene at this point and chase away the intruder, your cat is likely to respond with gratitude, licking your hands and face profusely. When this happens, he is saying thanks to you, his pack leader, for helping defend territory he regards as shared by you both.

Clicks

When hunting, cats often emit a repeated clicking sound intended to alert others in the pack that prey is nearby being stalked. Produced in irregular bursts, these clicks enable the cat to communicate with others without arousing their victim's suspicions. If you dislike the idea of the back garden being turned into a slaughterhouse for birds, be sure to call your cat indoors any time you hear these clicking signals.

How Kittens Talk

So far I have only discussed the sounds made by mature cats, but kittens also vocalize and it can be fascinating to study their calls and to see how they gradually increase an initially limited vocabulary by imitating older animals.

If you get the chance, try to make some recordings of a kitten's language development using the methods I shall be describing later.

Purring starts as early as the second day after birth, while the "mrhrhrhn" greeting appears around the third week of life, with other murmurs developing over the following weeks.

Listening to kittens attempting an aggressive spit for the first time can be amusing, since the "tff! tff! tff!" produced sounds more like a human than the cry of a cat.

When Cats Converse

It is difficult to be specific about exactly where and how a particular cat is likely to talk, since each is such an individual and, just like us, some chatter a great deal more than others. You may have a quiet, introverted pet who hardly utters or a gregarious, talkative extrovert animal who converses almost all the time.

Cats use their calls in a wide variety of situations, but here I shall describe the circumstances under which you are most likely to hear them talk and explain how sounds are used to deal with the humans, or other animals, involved.

Reward Seeking

These are situations in which your cat is striving to obtain some type of reward, perhaps food or a favorite toy. The importance attached to any particular goal is reflected in both the number and intensity of the calls. If you want to find out which of two kinds of food your cat really likes the best, show him both and then place them, one after the other, just out of reach. By comparing the frequency and loudness of his calls, you can easily tell which one is his favorite.

Calls for Your Attention

Cats reserve certain calls almost exclusively for talking to humans and expressing some need or emotion.

The greeting murmur is far more frequently directed toward humans than other cats, and used most often to greet somebody the cat knows well and is fond of. You are likely to hear it on returning home after a short absence, especially if you then start talking in a friendly way.

If you suspect that your cat feels ill, uncomfortable or generally under the weather, check your hunch by talking sympathetically and showing a lot of interest in him. If he responds with one of the complaining murmurs, your suspicions are probably justified.

Confidence

The amount of confidence your cat brings to a particular task is also reflected in his calls. If experience has taught him that calling is going to produce a successful outcome, then he will increasingly start to emphasize the initial "aaaah" component of the cry.

How Cats Talk to Cats

Most owners are only too familiar with the calls made by cats during the mating season. The female advertises her condition loudly and unmistakably, while males squabble over territory using typically caterwauling cries. Sexual invitations are issued using the coaxing murmur.

During pregnancy, the female conveys her desire for additional food, water and sympathy by the increased use of begging calls. When talking to her kittens, she uses soft "mhrhrn" murmuring calls and licks them according to a precise and genetically determined sequence.

Their loins and pelvic region receive the most affection, followed by the mouth, then the underbelly and finally the back and sides. (Licking also has important implications for the healing power of cats, a subject which we shall be looking at in the next chapter.)

When her kittens are old enough to leave the basket, she continues to use the same sort of murmur to attract their attention but increases its firmness and intensity. When inviting the kittens to play, she uses a softer, coaxing cry. If they fail to respond, however, the calls will become sterner and more complaining. Should their play become a little too rough, she may give voice to an anger call combined with some growling. In my experience, however, such signs of irritation seldom make much impression on a litter of boisterously playful kittens!

How Cats Talk with Their Bodies

When we speak, much of our message is communicated nonverbally, by facial expression, gesture, posture and gaze. Cats too make considerable use of these silent speech signals when conveying their feelings.

TAIL SIGNALS

The stiff upward flick: Made by the cat raising its tail straight up with a rapid motion until it is more or less vertical.

This greeting signal, which may be directed at both humans and other cats, is usually accompanied by a slightly arched back and either the "mrrrrt" or "mhrhrhrn" greeting murmur.

The overhead tail: You occasionally see a male cat walking around with his tail bent forward over his head. This is a dominance signal, used to tell the neighborhood females he's a top cat and to warn less assertive males to steer clear.

The switching tail: The most often observed signal, this consists of quick to-and-fro movements and is used to communicate annoyance. It is normally accompanied by other nonverbal signs of irritation and often by growling or an angry wail.

The randomly moving tail: Here the tail makes haphazard sweeping or twitching movements, usually while the cat is at rest, and indicates that although apparently relaxed he is still alert and ready for action. As he starts to get drowsy, tail movements become less expansive and finally cease entirely as he drops to sleep. The more alert your cat, the brisker his tail movements and the more space they occupy. Some especially lively cats never seem to stop moving their tails and you can learn a great deal about their moods by watching these movements.

EAR SIGNALS

Flattened ears: Another familiar signal, which often accompanies tail switching, it is a clear sign of annoyance.

Twitching ears: If your cat flicks his ears rapidly backwards and forwards a couple of times, he's conveying anxiety. You are likely to see this signal any time you scold your cat.

LIP LICKING

Another clear indication of mild worry or concern is when the cat gives *exactly* two quick licks while keeping a watchful eye on the human, animal or object which is worrying him. Other types of lip licking, such as one sees after the cat has eaten, are much more extensive and should not be confused with this very specific anxiety message.

THE GREETING HOP

A welcome signal made by cats as they approach somebody they like. This is performed by lifting the two front paws off the ground and setting them down again quickly while the legs are held stiff. It is often followed up by the cat rubbing himself against that person's legs.

THE HEAD BOW

Another greeting signal, this one is reserved almost exclusively for other cats. The head moves rapidly up and down, as if bowing to a monarch, and may turn slightly at the same time.

RAISED LIMP PAW

You sometimes see a cat suddenly stop and raise one front leg, relaxing the paw at the same moment so that it hangs limply. He may then appear to concentrate intently, as though attempting to identify a scent or sound. It tells you that something unexpected or puzzling has caught his interest and he is trying to find out what it was without betraying his own position by unnecessary movement. It's the equivalent of saying: "Hey, what was that?"

THE STOMACH DISPLAY

When offered either to humans or other cats, this is the ultimate signal of friendship and trust. The cat's stomach is usually defended aggressively, as you'll quickly discover should you be unwise enough to attempt to touch it without permission. Then the instinctive response to such uninvited familiarity is a display of teeth and claws. This is not a sign of viciousness, but a basic survival reflex acquired through evolution to safeguard the most vulnerable part of the animal's body.

When the trust between you and your cat is complete, however, he will roll over and offer his stomach. If inviting your caresses, the front legs will be held well back while the front paws are completely limp. This is your signal to move your hand slowly onto the stomach and give it a gentle pat. But approach carefully when this signal is apparently sent by a strange cat, because he could just be rolling over to rub his back, the way many animals do, and might resent your taking such liberties.

FACIAL EXPRESSIONS

The great ethologist Konrad Lorenz noted that "few animals display their mood via facial expressions as distinctly as cats." One of Lorenz's equally distinguished colleagues, Professor Paul Leyhausen, has made a detailed study of the cat's extensive repertoire of expressions and discovered that, unique among all the animals, cats are able to display two very different emotions—fear and aggression—at exactly the same time.

A cat may, for instance, simultaneously express agitation and fear responses ranging from the mild to the intense. Equally, he may show great fear accompanied by facial features indicating anything from total submission to considerable aggression. This chart allows you to monitor both these responses and interpret the full range of expressions shown.

Starting with the normal expression in the top left square, increasing attack threat is displayed as you move right, increasing defensiveness as you move downward. If you examine the leftmost column, you'll notice that the cat's ears shift from pointing straight up as the animal displays little fear to a flat position where the tips are curled upward as the cat becomes more frightened. This is because attackers signal their readiness to fight by exposing more of the backs of their ears.

The ears are used differently as aggression increases (from left to right across the rows), losing their curl and flattening straight down against the sides of the cat's head.

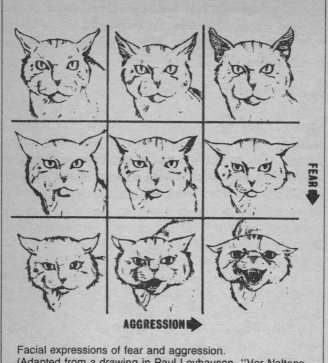

Facial expressions of fear and aggression.
(Adapted from a drawing in Paul Leyhausen, "Ver Naltens-
studien bei Katzen," *Zeitschrift für Tierpsychologie*, 1956.)

Flattening of the ears in this way indicates a readiness to
defend their territory, fight over the possession of a female,
protect a litter and so on.

Notice too how the pupils get larger, in both fear and
aggression, with the greatest dilation being seen in the
lower right-hand square where the cat displays each of these
two emotions with equal intensity. Exactly the same pro-
portions of fear and anger are also signaled by the cat's
body position.

Pupil enlargement is an important sign of arousal in both cats and humans, but need not necessarily have anything to do with either attack or defense. You can usually tell just how alert your cat is, or how much he likes some toy or tidbit, by observing the size of his pupils. The larger they are, the more alert he is and the more interested in what you have to offer. In the top picture, the wide-eyed look is combined with a dropped head, giving the cat a slightly "hunchbacked" appearance. If your cat adopts this posture while gazing intently at something, a human or another animal, he is expressing a strong "threat" by saying, in effect: "Don't mess with me or you'll be in trouble . . ."

Half-closed eyes, however, send a very friendly signal that conveys acceptance and affection. This is the signal you can easily use yourself while talking to your cat. By doing so you will further strengthen the bond of mutual love and trust.

POSTURE

The drawings below, based on my own and Professor Leyhausen's studies, show how fear/aggression signals are also conveyed via posture.

The normal body position is shown in the top left corner, with increased fear, and therefore defensiveness, depicted as you move from top to bottom. Greater aggression, and hence a tendency to attack, can be seen in the drawings moving from left to right. An important factor here is the distance between the cat's body and the ground.

The more aggressive a cat feels, the taller he will make himself. If fearful, on the other hand, he'll crouch as close to the ground as he can to make himself as small as possible.

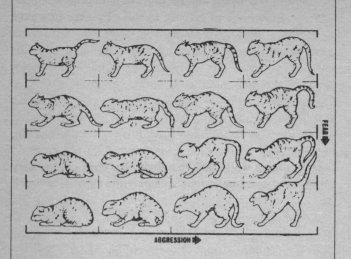

Bodily expressions of fear and aggression. In each row, fear increases downward and aggression from left to right. (Adapted from Leyhausen.)

SMELL SIGNALS

Like many animals, the cat uses his keen sense of smell, together with specially produced chemicals, to convey information to other animals. These chemicals are called pheromones, from two Greek words meaning to "convey" and to "urge on." As the name implies, a pheromone is a chemical used for communication between animals, and can be likened to hormones, which send chemical messages around the body.

When your cat rubs himself against your leg, for instance, you would be right to assume it's an expression of affection or a begging signal. But this action has an additional and more subtle purpose as well. Because cats have special odor-producing glands in the middle of the forehead and around the mouth and chin, rubbing their heads against something leaves behind a distinctive scent. This warns other cats that certain objects, places or people are their exclusive property and that any claims to ownership will be bitterly contested. This is the reason why cats occasionally seem to rub their heads over almost everything in sight.

Dog-owners well know that their pets stake out territory using urine as a marker. Cats employ the same tactic with one significant difference. Not only do the pheromones in their discharges create signposts indicating the borders of their territory, they also tell other cats how recently that territory was marked out.

Research by Dr. J. DeBoer at the Laboratory of Animal Physiology in Amsterdam has shown that this system enables several different cats to occupy the same area on a sort of time-sharing basis. As soon as a cat moves into new territory, he lays down markers to establish his rights over that piece of land. As time passes, the pheromones decay at a precise and steady rate, so indicating the passing of time like the ticking of a clock.

Dr. DeBoer discovered that four-hour-old markers were the first to be investigated by visiting cats and usually stopped them from claiming the territory as their own. The older the markers were, the less influence they exerted.

The general rule, therefore, seems to be that each cat can lay claim to an area and occupy it for up to four hours before being seriously challenged by another. In the wilderness, such a tactic would have considerable survival value by allowing several cats to hunt and search out mates in the same, often fairly limited, area.

But scents do more than merely identify an individual animal's territory. The entire route a cat has traveled is often carefully signposted with pheromones to allow others to follow the trail. Cats also tend to leave scent markers close to or even on the back door of their home to indicate that it is their "center of operations."

When you let your cat out after a period indoors, you may well see him investigating the garden carefully in search of scent trails laid down by intruders and only relaxing when satisfied that his territory has not been violated.

Scent markers can be laid down in two ways. First, your cat may simply rub himself against a series of objects along his favorite trails, so as to leave an odor on them. Alternately, he may wish to establish a more positive set of markers by rubbing the side of his chin against an object, perhaps curling his lip at the same time to increase the quantity of pheromones deposited.

Talking to Cats

Before you can start talking to cats, especially those you've only just met, it's essential to win their trust and confidence. If you notice a cat, your own or a stranger, watching you, never return their gaze since this conveys a threat in cat language. If the animal starts feeling threatened, you'll almost certainly notice such signs of anxiety as the ear twitch or the double lip lick, after which it will be very hard to open any dialogue between you.

Instead, while the cat is looking at your face, gradually sink down on your heels so as to come closer to his level. Remember that any cat sending out aggressive messages is going to raise itself from the ground, so you want to avoid giving the wrong impression.

Now look slowly away from the cat, before allowing your gaze to return to his face. As you do so, half close your eyes prior to restoring eye contact. Then, when you are looking at one another, blink several times. This reassurance signal when used by two cats will have the same result if used between a human and a cat. By adopting this opening gambit on several occasions, you should soon find the cat becomes increasingly eager to converse with you.

Once your approach has been accepted, the cat may acknowledge this trust by lowering his lids and blinking or by using one of the greeting signals already described.

To get on even better terms, use the head rub by placing your forehead against his and rubbing your nose and chin against his head. This is a warm and affectionate greeting message often used between two friendly cats.

If the cat has not yet fully accepted you, such an invitation to greater intimacy may be rejected, with the cat turning abruptly away or even walking off. If accepted, however, a very close bond will have been formed between you.

Spoken conversation can easily be established by making sure you use the same words and intonations on each occasion. When thinking about making his lunch, for example, you might ask if he actually wants food at that moment. As you make this request, show either the tin or the food on his plate. If interested, he will probably emit one of the demand calls. After you have repeated this approach on a few occasions, the cat will learn the meaning of those words and reply without being shown the food itself. You can, of course, adopt exactly the same procedure to discover if he wants to be petted, to play with a favorite toy, to go out and so on.

How to Get Cat Talk on Tape

As I explained at the start of this chapter, you may find it helpful to make a recording of cat calls and note the situations in which each one is used. This will help you to gain an even greater understanding of your cat's use of language.

You can do this using any kind of tape recorder, although you will find those with a separate microphone easier to use. Here are some hints for getting the best recordings.

1. You should be within no less than four feet of your cat, in a fairly quiet room. It also helps to kneel down, thus bringing yourself closer to the cat's level.

2. The type of microphone supplied with most domestic recorders is omnidirectional, which means it picks up sounds coming from all directions. Although this feature can be helpful for general recordings, it is usually a disadvantage when recording cat sounds, since unwanted and distracting noises may also be taped. There are two ways around this. You can purchase a microphone which detects sounds over a narrower area and which will help to cut down such distractions, although you'll have to position it carefully to ensure that the calls are clearly recorded. Any good stereo store can advise you about the most suitable microphone for your particular tape recorder. Alternatively, use an omnidirectional microphone but place it as close to your cat as possible. If making recordings indoors, shut out unwanted background noise by closing the cur-

tains, turning off the TV, asking your family to keep quiet for a time and, perhaps, taking the phone off the hook. Use the longest possible lead so that the tape recorder can be hidden from sight. At first, the microphone alone will probably intrigue your cat, who will insist on playing with it and exploring it. Let him get used to it before trying to make any serious recordings.

3. Many recorders allow you to adjust the level at which sounds are recorded. When taping cats for the first time, there is a tendency to turn up this control as far as possible in the hope of catching the slightest sounds. However, this causes much of the recording to be made at too high a level, resulting in distortion, which may make it difficult to identify the more subtle features of a particular cry.

   Set the level so that it never goes into the red portion of the readout or indicates in some other way that the input is excessive. The instruction book supplied with your machine will explain this point.

4. Use a good quality tape. It's worth the extra money to ensure the best reproduction your recorder can produce. Remember that many of the calls you will be recording are subtle and you'll need the best recording possible in order to identify the various shades of meaning they contain. Keep a careful log of each call, noting the situation in which the call was made. When you have a reasonable collection, compare them with the descriptions I have given of the different types of sounds used.

Learning the language of cats may occasionally prove frustrating and it certainly demands time and patience, but by doing so you will enjoy a far greater insight into the life of your pet and make the cat's life more interesting and agreeable too. After all, nothing is more annoying than not being able to make yourself understood by somebody of whom you are fond, and that applies to cats just as much as people.

There could be a practical advantage to such knowledge as well, for the occasion might arise when you would like your pet to play the part of family physician.

CHAPTER 4

The Healing Power of Cats

The drunken driver who sent little Maria spinning from her new bicycle sentenced the ten-year-old Mexican girl to a living death. In that moment of tragedy, a lively youngster was transformed into a helpless coma victim, unable to speak or move. After months in a hospital, the doctors suggested she be nursed at home as they could do nothing more for her.

Maria might have remained in her state of unconsciousness had it not been for the chance arrival of a stray cat, which the family named Miguel.

When I visited the family in their comfortable home on the outskirts of Mazatlan, on the Pacific Coast, Maria was playing happily with a handsome black cat. But that was not Miguel, her mother, Fransesca, told me. For, with his errand of mercy successfully completed, he had vanished into the warm Mexican night as silently and as mysteriously as he had first appeared.

Fransesca explained that she had first noticed the young cat when she went into her daughter's bedroom for a last time before going to bed. It was July 27, 1976, a date neither she nor her husband will ever forget. For at 11:30 that night their daughter took her first, faltering step along the road back to life.

"The room was dark," her mother recalled, "but a movement suddenly caught my eye. Close to my daughter's left hand, which rested outside the covers, was a small cat. My husband had left the window open because Maria had always loved the fresh air and her doctors had told us that any reminder of the past might awaken her."

Maria's bed was on the ground floor and her mother assumed that the thin, dirty stray had wandered in while searching for food. Horrified, Fransesca was on the point of lifting him from the bed when she saw something that made her call out to her husband in excitement. The cat was curled comfortably on the bed, his head close to the little girl's left wrist, patiently licking her thumb. As she noticed this, Fransesca observed something else as well— Maria's fingers were twitching slightly under the delicate caress. It was the first movement her mother had seen since the accident. Unconcerned by the woman's presence, the cat kept up his slow, purposeful licking and the girl's fingers moved once more, this time with greater vigor.

After that night Miguel, as they called him, was not simply allowed to sleep in the child's bedroom. He was positively encouraged. Sometimes he disappeared via the window (Miguel never entered or left the bedroom through the door), but always returned within a few hours. Most of the time he spent snuggled up to the girl, patiently grooming her fingers with his pink tongue.

Eight days after Miguel's arrival, Maria emerged from her coma and spoke for the first time in almost seven months. From then on, recovery was rapid. When she was fully recovered, her parents decided to take her on a vacation to the United States. Their housekeeper was given strict instructions to leave the bedroom window open and place fresh food and milk beside the bed each evening. But when they returned from their trip two weeks later, Miguel had vanished.

According to the housekeeper, he came back to the house on four nights in succession, ate the food and slept on the empty bed. But when she went into the room on the fifth day, the woman found the food untouched and the bedspread undisturbed. They never saw Miguel again.

Maria was thirteen when I met her, and still devoted to cats. They have had two since her almost miraculous return to health—both black and both called Miguel.

Maria's recovery, although remarkable, would not come as a complete surprise to the increasing number of physicians and psychiatrists around the world who have had firsthand experience of the almost miraculous healing power of cats. Their studies have shown that caring for, and loving, a cat provides more than emotional satisfaction. It also safeguards physical health and may even help to save life.

So important have they proved in some forms of treatment that cats are now being bred with temperaments and personalities precisely tailored to the demands of therapy.

About eighteen months after I visited Maria and her parents in Mexico, I was standing in the rather gloomy ward of a mental hospital on the outskirts of Washington, D.C. But if the surroundings—olive green walls, brown curtains and iron-framed beds—gave an appearance of drabness, there could be no mistaking the enthusiasm and dedication of the medical and nursing staff. I had been invited by the chief psychiatrist to observe the start of what would, he hoped, become a close and mutually rewarding friendship.

Maria and Miguel had met through the accident of an open bedroom window. Billy, a nineteen-year-old seriously ill mental patient, was about to be deliberately introduced to his new friend, a fifteen-month-old marmalade cat named Rocky.

During Billy's years in hospital, all kinds of pills and potions had failed to bring about any improvement in his condition. Now the psychiatrist was hoping that the healing powers of a cat might open windows on a long-shuttered mind.

Billy, severely autistic since early childhood, spent his days motionless in the hospital bed, staring unblinkingly at the only thing in the world which seemed to hold any interest for him, a zig-zag crack on the opposite wall. Nurses fed him, bathed him and changed his linen. If, during these chores, they happened to move him so that he could no longer see the crack, he would emit a series of high-pitched shrieks until he was able to fix his gaze on it again. Those screams were his only way of communicating with the world.

The psychiatrist carried the cat into Billy's ward and placed him on the young man's bed.

"This is Rocky," he said quietly. "I know you two will become good friends."

Billy's eyes moved briefly from the crack on the wall to give the cat a rapid, disinterested glance. Undeterred, the psychiatrist took Billy's hand and held it before Rocky's nose. After sniffing the limp fingers carefully for a moment, the cat gave a few greeting licks before settling down with his head resting on the young man's arm.

Although their first meeting appeared to have left little impression on Billy, a bond of friendship did, very slowly, develop during the days and weeks which followed. At first Billy had to be coaxed into petting the cat. A nurse would take his hand and move the unresponsive fingers through Rocky's long sleek coat. Gradually, perhaps affected by the animal's obvious enjoyment, Billy began to take an active interest in caressing him and did so without any encouragement. In time he learned to feed, look after and, finally, to play games with the cat.

The breakthrough his doctors had been hoping for came on the day he turned to a nurse and said quietly: "Rocky's hungry, he wants some food."

They were the first words he had spoken for more than a decade. From then on progress was swift. A few months afterward he was well enough to leave the hospital and go home to his parents.

Today Billy is attending a special school but proving to be an intelligent young man, and he is starting to make up for the lost years. Needless to say, he and Rocky remain the best of friends.

How Cats Heal

Since cats' ability to soothe sick minds and comfort sick bodies was first recognized, during the mid-1970s, they have become increasingly important in therapy and have found a caring role not only in hospitals but also in schools for the handicapped, drug and alcohol addiction units, and rest homes. They have helped men, women and children afflicted with such diverse problems as mental illness, heart disease, and brain damage caused by strokes or accidental injury. They have assisted in keeping alcoholics off the bottle and encouraged drug addicts to kick the habit.

Among the first therapists to recognize the benefits of cats were those working at Green Chimneys, a special public school for disturbed and handicapped children in Brewster, New York. Founded in 1948, Green Chimneys currently has around 140 two-legged residents and five times as many four-legged ones, ranging from cats to calves and pigs to ponies.

The children, most of whom come from large cities, tend these creatures as an active and important part of their rehabilitation or treatment program. John Gaines, the school's director, says that this caring does more than provide the youngsters with an interest and a responsibility. Working with animals, he says, exerts "a calming, soothing effect on children whose inner life is frantic and tumultuous."

Fifteen years ago many childcare specialists would have dismissed such ideas as improbable and regarded the Green Chimney menagerie as little more than a gimmick. Today the vast majority of healthcare specialists are convinced that pets of all kinds can be of tremendous therapeutic benefit, although some animals are much better suited to the role than others. At the top of the list, in the opinion of many specialists, comes the cat.

Pioneers of this form of treatment are Drs. Samuel and Elizabeth Corson and their colleagues in the Department of Psychiatry at Ohio State University. They believe their pets "act as a catalyst for feelings which are eventually transferred to other people." They also provide an outlet for emotions which might otherwise remain blocked. Many patients, for example, are able to accept affection from a cat long before they can respond to it in humans. In this way the pet serves as a bridge between the outright rejection and gradual acceptance of personal relationships. "When they play with cats, and other pets, even the seriously ill become different people," says Professor Corson. "They receive the kind of love which helps them most."

Dr. Gerald Lowbeer, a consultant psychiatrist at Horton Hospital in Epsom, England, considers that pets help in another way as well. He points out that, no matter how well they are looked after in a hospital, patients feel humiliated by their total dependency on the medical and nursing staff. Caring for a cat restores lost confidence and rebuilds self-esteem by allowing the patients to become active care-givers instead of being obliged always to play the role of passive care-receivers. They take responsibility for the life of another creature and receive, in return, its devotion, gratitude and affection.

Dr. James Serpell, of the Department of Animal Behavior at Cambridge University, explains what happens in the language of science when he comments that cats and some other pets possess a "repertoire of anthropomorphic signals . . . which if directed by one human being towards another would unmistakably indicate intense and unequivocal love and admiration." In other words, through the use of those potent silent speech signals we examined in the last chapter, cats are able to convey deep and positive feelings toward those who care for them.

An ardent supporter of this view is Dr. Marcel Heiman, attending psychiatrist at the Mount Sinai Hospital in New York City. He insists that cat therapy can work where other forms of treatment have been dismal failures. In many cases of mental disturbance he has found that a pet may represent the "only and last lifeline" back to reality.

In 1954, delegates from many parts of the world who attended the world's first Symposium on Pets and Society in Toronto, Canada, listened as speaker after speaker described how animals helped to satisfy dependency needs, serve as child substitutes to those unable to have children, provide companionship to the lonely and give love which has no strings attached.

One of those specialists who presented papers at the conference, an eminent American psychologist with the rather appropriate name of Dr. Michael Fox, told a fascinated audience how learning to love a pet makes people kinder and more sympathetic toward human suffering.

Many of the early studies used dogs rather than cats as the chosen animal. When Samuel and Elizabeth Corson first introduced animals into the treatment of mental illness, for example, they used various breeds of dog in an attempt to help fifty long-stay mental patients who had failed to respond to traditional forms of therapy. All but three accepted the pets happily and began to show a striking improvement almost immediately. One man soon started talking again after a silence which had lasted for more than twenty-six years.

Another psychiatrist, Dr. Boris Levinson, also used mainly dogs when he developed a pet-oriented child psychotherapy for the diagnosis and treatment of psychologically disturbed youngsters. On the basis of this research, and from their personal experience, dog-owners might conclude that this loving, affable animal would always prove a better therapist than the more aloof, far less dependent cat. Dogs are, after all, renowned for their friendliness, desire to please, and warm, affectionate nature.

In fact, it is their independent nature which tends to make cats more effective in the healing role. Dr. Marcel Heiman points out that the dog's sensitivity and responsiveness to human emotions can make it vulnerable to an owner's emotional distress. This may mean, for example, that a neurotic owner can unintentionally pass on his fears to the pet. After examining a large number of dogs with behavior problems, Dr. Daniel Tortora, one of America's foremost animal psychologists, has concluded that they are usually only acting out their master's or mistress's hangups. "In each of these cases," he says, "the pet's behavior problem is a symptom of a less obvious but potentially more serious psychological problem in its owner."

Although the same tendency can, occasionally, be found in cats, Dr. Heiman stresses that this rarely causes difficulties during treatment. "The cat and his owner enjoy an entirely different sort of relationship," he explains.

The important part played by cats in the lives of their owners may be enhanced even further by an additional consideration. As the research by Aline and Robert Kidd (described in Chapter One) showed, more cat- than dog-owners expressed a dislike for children. Many psychotherapists believe that cats, and indeed other pets, can become a substitute child, evoking feelings which would otherwise be aroused by human infants.

But therapists have also found that while all cats possess this power to enhance the healing process, some, because of their particularly sensitive temperaments and warm personalities, prove far more effective than others. Rocky, the cat who worked a minor miracle with Billy, for example, was specially bred to ensure that he would be extremely affectionate and responsive. This process involves selecting suitable cats by carefully observing how they behave toward humans and then breeding from those who display the greatest warmth, affection and empathy. After several generations, a cat is produced with a character perfectly in tune with the emotional needs of the sick.

So far we have only looked at the cat's powers to soothe the sick, but they can also exert an extremely beneficial influence in maintaining health.

The first hint of this unexpected link between owning cats and enjoying better health came about in 1977 through the work of Drs. Aaron Katcher and Erica Friedmann at the University of Pennsylvania. In order to study the effects of loneliness on recovery from heart attacks, they gathered together nearly a hundred men and women who were recovering from such an attack and gave them a detailed physical and psychological examination. They also assessed their life-styles by asking them to complete a questionnaire which included a few items concerning the ownership of pets.

Twelve months later, Katcher and Friedmann contacted the patients again to see how they had fared. Fourteen of the group had died over the year, but the remainder were in good health. A statistical analysis was then made of the interview data to establish any common pattern among the survivors.

What emerged surprised the researchers and caused considerable interest among doctors and specialists when Dr. Friedmann reported their findings at a conference of the American Heart Association in Dallas, Texas. Allowing for such factors as the severity of the attacks, clear evidence had been found to show that owning a pet could mean the difference between living and dying.

To identify just what it was about pet ownership that proved so beneficial to health, Katcher and Friedmann asked volunteers to bring their pets into the laboratory. There the owners were wired to a wide variety of electronic biofeedback equipment which continuously monitored such aspects of body function as blood pressure, heart rate, respiration and the ability of the skin to conduct minute electric currents. This last measure provides a very sensitive indication of anxiety, since the more aroused we become, the more we sweat and the more efficient a conductor our skin becomes.

After being attached to the monitoring devices, the owners were instructed to stroke, talk and play with their pets and generally to enjoy their company.

Despite the clinical surroundings, blood pressure, heart

rate and skin conductivity all declined significantly as soon as the subjects started to caress their pets. Simply fondling a much-loved cat or affectionate dog was enough to reduce physical arousal to a point which is often attained only after weeks of practice in relaxation or meditation procedures.

The healing power of cats is not confined to human patients, as I discovered a few years ago when I first visited a remarkable animal sanctuary run by Elizabeth Stuart-Hogg on the south coast of England. At her home in the shadow of a Norman castle, Elizabeth has cared for hundreds of injured birds and animals over the past twenty years, tending their wounds and patiently nursing them back to health. When I called, the sick bay included an owl with an injured wing, a baby hedgehog, a guillemot with oiled-up feathers and a parrot with a broken leg. Elizabeth was caring for them all, but she was not working alone. Playing an active part in the healing process were four of her many cats: Percy, who was looking after Gillette the guillemot; Simeon, who was napping with Timothy the hedgehog; William, who had adopted Buffy the owl; and Whisper, the best friend of Guppy the parrot.

While the injured animals remained in the sanctuary—a stay which could vary from a few days to several weeks—these cats played an active role in helping them regain their health. One of the most remarkable sights I saw at any time during my investigations was Percy patiently grooming Gillette's feathers while William lay asleep beside an owl.

"My cats are natural healers," Elizabeth told me, "and they tend for the sick animals who are brought here every bit as carefully as I do. I am sure without their help many who make excellent recoveries might not even survive."

So what power does the cat possess that makes it such a successful healer? Their success is certainly not just due to providing patients with warm, responsive and undemanding companionship. Valuable though this undoubtedly is, the specialists I talked to agreed that the healing power has much deeper roots and is due, to a considerable extent, to the unique psychological bond which develops between patient and pet.

Because cats are so much more independent than other pets, their favors tend to prove even more rewarding. You know that when a cat accepts and loves you, the bond is very special and is valued all the more for this reason. And with cats, all expressions of love are open and honest. Unlike humans, they never lie or flatter when they convey their affections by the silent signals—rubbing themselves gently against your body, arching their necks under your caress, licking your fingers and so on.

Which brings me to the second reason why cats prove so effective as therapists. They are experts at using, and responding to, touch. In Western culture, especially, physical contact between adults is actively discouraged and many therapists believe that we are all the worse for this taboo.

"Touching, like being called by first name, is considered an act of intimacy, a privilege usually granted only to those of one's own class or status whom one has allowed to pass across those social barriers which serve to exclude the underprivileged," comments Dr. Ashley Montagu in his book *Touching*.

The potency of tactile stimulation becomes easy to understand when one realizes the extreme sensitivity of the skin. The largest organ in the body, it covers some 18 square feet in an adult, weighs around 8 lbs. and constitutes between 6 and 8 percent of total body weight. Every square inch contains in excess of 6 million cells and 100 nerve endings, making a total of more than 640,000 sensory receptors over the entire skin surface.

Indeed, the skin is the body's most crucial sensory system. We could survive, and even overcome to a great extent, handicaps caused by the loss of sight, hearing, taste and smell. But if deprived of our tactile sense, life would become impossible. Without the continuous feedback which the skin provides, for example, the brain cannot adjust muscle tone to respond to external conditions. When an arm or leg "goes to sleep," the lack of sensory input makes it very hard to move the affected limb because vital signals are no longer getting through. Even during deep sleep, feedback from the skin must be maintained constantly. As Bertrand Russell commented, "Our whole conception of what exists outside us is based upon the sense of touch."

Satisfying the sense of touch is, therefore, vitally important to our physical and emotional health. Yet from our earliest years many of us are starved of this form of stimulation.

Anthropologist Margaret Mead once pointed out that while a Western baby is being bathed, a time when tactile stimulation might be at its maximum, the infant's attention is deliberately distracted from the intimacy of touch by placing toys in the tub. "The average American woman may never hold a little baby until she nurses her own," said Margaret Mead. "And even then she often behaves at though she were still afraid the infant might break in her hands."

In their 1963 study of a New England town, the American psychologists Drs. J. L. and A. Fischer found that most babies spent a good part of each day on their own in playpen or crib, and reported that "such contact as a baby has with other human beings is not marked by close bodily contact as in many societies."

In adulthood, this deprivation frequently creates serious emotional barriers either to touching or being touched by others. Instead of this activity being viewed as normal, natural and, indeed, highly desirable, it is considered only proper—apart from family and intimate friends—in a limited number of carefully controlled circumstances, such as while being treated by a doctor or nurse, receiving physiotherapy, having one's hair cut or nails manicured and so on.

Most humans, especially those experiencing some form of psychological breakdown or emotional hangup, are touch-deprived. Studies have shown, for example, that parents who batter or otherwise abuse their children were themselves battered and abused in childhood and only rarely report having had a pet.

As one advocate of touch therapy, Dr. Bertram Forer, puts it: "The primitive reaction to being touched gently at critical periods is a feeling of body relaxation and reassurance that one is not alone, that old feelings of unworthiness are not justified."

Certain types of animals can, however, fill this need in a nonthreatening way, as the word "pet," which can also mean to stroke, fondle or caress, implies. And where cats are concerned, the mutual caressing takes a very distinctive and particularly effective form.

Animals lick their young not just to clean them but, far more importantly, to keep the various systems of the body—circulatory, digestive, nervous, reproductive and so on—in peak condition through constant stimulation. When hand-rearing an orphaned kitten, for example, it is essential to do more than merely provide food. Without appropriate stimulation, provided by a cotton swab dipped in warm water, the animal is unable to eliminate bodily waste. As I explained in the last chapter, a female cat licks her kittens in a precise sequence determined by an inborn program which also fixes the rate of licking at between three to four per second. Cats spend up to 53 percent of their time engaged in this task, a concentration of effort far greater than that devoted to any other activity.

With grooming forming such a vital part of the cat's behavior, it is not surprising to find that the feline tongue has evolved a special surface consisting of three different kinds of projections to aid this important process. Among the most important and numerous are the threadlike papillae found mainly along the central area at the tongue's free end. Horny and toothlike, with rear-facing points, it is these filiform papillae which produce the rasping that accompanies a cat's friendly licks of greeting.

So here we have a touch therapist uniquely qualified to satisfy the basic human need for tactile stimulation, a creature whose primitive nature is to groom using a tongue which can apply a subtle but powerful form of grooming to the surface of the skin and which accepts, in return, the gentle massaging of its own soft, warm and extremely touch-satisfying body.

You will recall how both Maria and Billy, though otherwise seemingly unaware of the world around them, responded very rapidly as the cat's tongue gently caressed their fingers. This response is easier to understand when one appreciates the connection between skin stimulation and brain activity.

Not only is the skin the body's largest organ but its various elements are extremely well represented in the brain, with large quantities of gray matter being allocated to processing signals from the hand, and especially the fingers and the thumb. It is hardly surprising, therefore, that the skin is a highly sensitive barometer which warns of internal emotional turmoil by producing such stress-related disorders as sores, eczema, boils, psoriasis and urticaria. Nor is it remarkable that touch should have such an important part to play in our overall well-being.

When the cat obeys an instinct to safeguard the health of bodily systems through the act of grooming, therefore, it brings a healing touch both to its own kind, to other animals and to humans. In return, the cat relishes being stroked and encourages such grooming with purrs of delight. This action not only brings pleasure to the animal but helps us to satisfy our own unfulfilled tactile needs. At the same time, the cat's independent nature protects it against the fears and emotional turmoil of the owner.

The healing power of cats is a wonderful example of the helpful, caring role these animals play in their relationship with the human race. But this is not the only way in which humans can derive great benefit from their companionship and affection. Cats can also help to save life and prevent injury through their uncanny talent for foretelling the future.

CHAPTER 5

When Cats Foresee the Future

During World War II, radar towers along Britain's south coast scanned the air over France for incoming squadrons of Nazi bombers, while listening posts and skilled observers probed the skies for the sights and sounds that meant another raid was about to begin.

But many householders quickly discovered that an even more sensitive and reliable danger early warning system could be found curled up on their own hearth mats.

Cats, it was soon recognized, possessed an uncanny talent for predicting when death and destruction were about to rain down from the skies. Not only did many begin to show unmistakable signs of agitation and fear before the sirens even sounded, but they also seemed to know whether a particular family was in danger. Their hair would stand on end, they emitted the "chchchchch" or spit or anger wail, and a few even headed straight for the nearest shelter.

During the blitz this ability to foretell the future proved

of such great survival value that a special medal, engraved
with the words "We Also Serve," was awarded to pets
whose actions had helped to save lives.

One of them, a black-and-white cat called Sally who
lived close to the London docks, evolved an elaborate system for raising the alarm and getting her owner, and a
neighbor, down to the safety of their backyard Anderson
shelter before the bombs began to fall.

When sensing that a raid was about to start, Sally raced
to the stand in the hall and leaped urgently at the gas mask
hanging there, then darted back to her mistress and pawed
her excitedly. Next she would run into the yard and scratch
at the shelter entrance. Once her owner had taken refuge,
Sally jumped over the wall into the neighbor's yard, meowing loudly to attract her attention. Only when all three of
them were snug in the shelter would Sally finally relax,
curl up and go back to sleep.

Cats with young also used their predictive powers to
ensure the safety of their kittens. A woman who spent the
war years in Plymouth told me how, a considerable time
before the sirens wailed, her cat would carefully pick up
each of her litter in turn and carry the squirming kittens out
of her basket in the front room to the security of the cellar.

An even more remarkable story was reported to me from
Portsmouth, also a major *Luftwaffe* target. On one occasion
a cat had been shut up in a house, with her kittens, while
the owners were away at work. Sensing imminent danger,
she desperately searched the house for a way of escape and
finally discovered a partially open back bedroom window.
The drop into the garden was too great to risk, and there
was no convenient drainpipe or nearby tree to use as a
ladder. Then the resourceful cat noticed that a telephone
line connected up to the house close to the window, and
this thin cable became her lifeline. Lifting the kittens out

of their basket in the kitchen, she carried them upstairs one by one, and then onto the window-ledge. Next she leapt nimbly onto the line and balanced there, a protesting kitten held firmly by the scruff of the neck, before stalking, as calmly and confidently as any high-wire artist, to the telegraph pole. From there she scrambled down into the garden and placed the kitten on an old piece of sacking in the garden shed. With that rescue mission concluded, she then retraced her precarious route into the house to carry another of her young out of the house. Soon after the last kitten had been transported safely from the house, a bomb fell nearby and the house was badly damaged by the blast. The kitchen in which the cat and her kittens had been lying was showered with a fusillade of jagged glass and fragments of falling plaster. If the cat had not somehow foreseen the danger, it seems certain that all would have been seriously, perhaps fatally, injured.

But it has to be admitted that not all cats used their powers quite so nobly.

A Sussex family was surprised when their cat, Timothy, failed to join them in the shelter after the siren alerted them to a lunchtime raid. When the all clear sounded, however, his absence was explained. The cat, who usually had to make do on a diet of cheap fish scraps, had discovered four flounder dinners on the table. Perhaps Timothy was able to predict that neither he nor the house were in any danger because, scorning the safety of the shelter, he remained behind and ate them all!

These wartime stories offer a dramatic illustration of some of the ways in which cats appear to be able to foretell the future and forecast danger in ways which appear to defy rational explanation. In fact, however, there are perfectly reasonable theories for explaining many, if not all, of their predictive powers.

But this does not make them any less remarkable, or any less helpful to man. For, as we have already seen, cats frequently use their predictive talents to help safeguard human life. Sometimes their forecasts occur just before some major natural disaster or prior to a serious accident. Much more frequently, however, their predictions are far more mundane and concerned with such relatively trivial events as changes in the weather or the arrival of an unexpected guest. Indeed, once you know what to watch out for and can recognize the changes in a cat's behavior that might have some prophetic quality to it, you may be able to use your pet as a living crystal ball and, perhaps, prevent some misfortune from befalling your family.

So let's investigate the ways in which cats employ their predictive powers, examine some of the many case histories which illustrate their abilities in action and then see how science attempts to explain them.

How Cats Forecast the Weather

People who earn a living from either the land or the sea have long considered that cats can predict changes in the weather and other natural events of vital importance to them. Along the French coast, for instance, many fishermen and their families believe that:

- If a cat passes a paw behind an ear while grooming his muzzle it is going to rain.
- If he cleans his nose it is going to be windy.
- If his pupils are small it is low tide.
- If his pupils are wide it is high tide.
- If cats twist or turn it is the end of bad weather.

- If they turn their backs to the fire there will be a shipwreck.

One person who prefers to depend on her cat's forecasts rather than those of highly paid TV weatherpeople is Mrs. Freda Robinson of Oklahoma City. In his book, *The Psychic Powers of Animals*, author Bill Schul recounts how the behavior of Mrs. Robinson's cat, Felix, provides an infallible weather guide. When the day is going to be fine, he settles down on the windowsill, but if wet and stormy conditions lie ahead then he takes refuge on top of the family wardrobe, and, according to Freda, he never blunders.

A Kansas farmer, living outside the town of Lawrence, recalls how his cat not only predicted a tornado but even knew which buildings lay in its path of destruction. The mother of four kittens, she was caring for them in a barn close to his farmhouse. One afternoon he noticed that one of the kittens was missing, the next day a second had disappeared and then a third, until the whole family had vanished. On the night the last kitten was removed, a tornado struck the area, completely destroying the barn. The following morning, friends from a farm miles away called to see how much damage the storm had caused. They also came to return his cat and four kittens who had spent the past few days camped out in their own barn. The mother had obviously carried them across several miles of countryside to the safety of a building which, in some strange way, she knew would survive the tornado.

Hòw Cats Predict Events at Home

Many owners credit their cats with the ability to foretell the return of a well-liked owner by playing with unusual energy immediately prior to their arrival. Another told me how she always knew if visitors were going to call unexpectedly because her cat made a point of going into the dining room to clean itself.

In Washington, an eminent and very down-to-earth woman lawyer told me how her cat, General Jackson, always knew whether a phone call would bring good or unwelcome news. When the phone rang, he would immediately either put his nose against the receiver, in which case the call would invariably turn out well, or stalk haughtily out of the room, which meant that bad tidings could be expected. I was assured that in the three years since he had started this behavior, General Jackson had very seldom been wrong.

In the north of England I met Barney, a cat who simply loved television—not for its entertainment value but as a warm place on which to sleep. While his owner watched the screen, the ginger tom lay curled contentedly on top. Normally he climbed onto his perch as soon as the family sat down and stayed snoozing peacefully until the set was switched off for the night. One evening, however, he woke suddenly from a deep slumber and jumped to the floor. After standing and glaring at the flickering screen for a few moments, he bounded to the door and demanded to be allowed out. Not long afterwards the tube disintegrated and showered the room with shrapnel-like fragments of shattered glass. If Barney had stayed where he was, the chances are he would have been badly hurt.

Cats Who Save Human Life

A recurrent theme of cat predictions is the way in which they are often used to help humans in distress. Few tales I have heard make this point better than that of Riki, the cat who saved a girl from drowning.

Lola Del-Costa and her husband Ernesto, a qualified pilot, decided to fly in his private plane from their home in Italy for a Spanish honeymoon. After the wedding breakfast they took off from Milan airport with ample fuel aboard the small aircraft for the four-hour flight. But with safe landfall only thirty minutes away, and while they were still flying over the Mediterranean, disaster struck. First came strong headwinds, which slowed them down, reducing reserves of fuel to a dangerously low level. Then, abruptly, the engine cut out and they were forced to make an emergency landing on the water.

"We were thrown against the windshield and Ernesto was cut on the throat, but he kept calm, told me to jump into the sea and then followed me," Lola recalled.

They swam for some hours, with Ernesto growing weaker and weaker from loss of blood. Finally, knowing he would drown, he called out to Lola: "Courage. Save yourself." As she tried desperately to reach him, Ernesto slid from sight beneath the waves.

The pilot's final SOS had been picked up by a number of vessels which converged on the area to search for wreckage and survivors. Among them was the *Lattuga*, an Italian cargo ship, captained by forty-six-year-old Diego Suni. As the warm evening slowly faded into the pitch dark of a Mediterranean night, most of those aboard started to abandon any hope of finding the young couple alive. The Mayday signal had been sent out more than three hours earlier, and they had already searched a wide area without success.

The crew, lining the rails and peering into the shimmering patches of light as their vessel's powerful spotlights momentarily illuminated the waters, were already thinking of resuming their interrupted voyage when Riki, the ship's cat, suddenly darted to the prow, where he began meowing loudly while running excitedly back and forth.

Acting on a hunch, Captain Suni ordered the spotlights to be swung toward the prow. A few moments later they picked up a pale blob on the sea's surface. It was Lola's blonde hair streaming out across the black waters a hundred yards away.

Immediately, deckhand Walter Giuliotto pulled off his clothes and dived into the sea. Ten minutes later, shocked and exhausted by her ordeal but otherwise unharmed, Lola was being lifted gently aboard. She owed her life not only to the young seaman's bravery but to Riki's remarkable powers.

The desire of cats to use their powers to help humans is well illustrated by the following stories from America, Australia and Italy.

The Cat Who Saved a Baby

One bitterly cold winter's night, Virgil McMillian found a starving cat on the front porch of his home near the Arkansas town of Berryville. Picking up the bundle of shivering fur, he took it to the warmth of his stove and began nursing it back to health. Slowly Cat, as Virgil and his wife Linda named him, quickly regained his strength, and stayed on to become their affectionate pet. Every night, Slowly Cat was allowed out but always returned home within a few minutes. On an especially cold winter's night, however, some two years after he arrived, Slowly Cat went out and stayed out. With temperatures plunging to 12 degrees below zero, an anxious Virgil and Linda searched the frost-covered grounds around their home without success. Finally, they admitted defeat and went sadly to bed, hoping that Slowly Cat would somehow survive and return home to them.

When the couple woke next day, Slowly Cat was still missing and they began their hunt again. Searching around at the rear of their home, Virgil came across an old sack. He was about to throw it aside when the cat suddenly crawled out, stared unblinkingly at his master, and then wriggled back again.

Opening the sack carefully, Virgil stared in shocked amazement at the sight which met his eyes. A tiny, half-naked baby boy was lying at the bottom of the sack, with Slowly Cat curled around him and vigorously licking the infant's deathly pale face.

Virgil rushed the baby into the house and phoned for an ambulance. At Berryville Hospital the almost frozen infant was placed in charge of Dr. Alan Randolph. "The child's temperature had fallen to 94 degrees," he remembers. "We put him in an incubator and used special lamps to warm him up."

Slowly Cat had undoubtedly saved the abandoned baby from freezing to death on the frost-covered ground. "He could have died," says Dr. Randolph, "if the cat had not snuggled into the sack with him. The licking and the animal's body heat helped keep that child alive."

But what none of those involved in the drama were ever able to explain was how Slowly Cat knew that a baby had been abandoned in that old sack. Certainly the child had not been crying or Virgil and Linda would have heard him during their late-night search for their cat. Scent is a possibility, although the experts I talked to believed that the iron-hard ground would have made it difficult for the cat to pick up any scent. All that can be said is that, somehow, Slowly Cat was able to predict what he would find in that tattered scrap of burlap and, having discovered the baby, also realized that its life depended on the warmth of his body and the caress of his tongue.

The Cat Who Prevented a Murder

Sally is an Australian actress now living in London. Late one Friday night, some five years ago, she was returning to her Sydney home after working late at the television studios. The darkened street appeared deserted as she hurried the last few blocks to her apartment.

Although she was not normally an anxious person, Sally's nerves had been on edge for the past few weeks because a maniac murderer was known to be on the prowl, strangling women and then suspending their corpses from street lamps. All of the previous eight victims had been women around Sally's age and similar in appearance.

With the sanctuary of her front door just a block away, Sally began to breathe a little more easily. Suddenly she was startled to hear the loud and unmistakable sound of her cat, Caramel, meowing frantically in the darkness nearby.

This surprised her because, although able to come and go at will through a cat flap, the five-year-old tabby usually awaited her return from the comfort of a favorite armchair.

With the cries getting closer, Sally paused so that Caramel could catch up with her. As she did so, a powerful hand seemed to come from nowhere and fasten like a steel trap around her throat. Unable to cry out, and with her strength rapidly failing, Sally felt herself being dragged toward a car parked at the curbside. Then, out of the corner of her eye, she noticed her cat racing toward them down the pavement, still calling loudly.

Catching sight of the animal, and momentarily startled by the noise, her attacker loosened his grip on her windpipe for a moment—just long enough for Sally to let out an ear-splitting scream of terror.

The killer, now alarmed, immediately released her, jumped into the car and roared away down the street. Later the police told Sally that she was extremely lucky to be alive. They had no doubt that the killer had cast her in the role of victim number nine and commented that her deafening scream had saved her life. Sally, however, knew that her real savior was Caramel. Somehow she appeared to have foretold the attack and done her utmost to save her mistress from the murderer.

So far we have looked at cases where cats used their powers to predict threats to individuals. But there are also many occasions in which their forecasts have helped to save whole communities from death and injury by alerting them to the imminent danger of some natural disaster.

Cats Who Predict Disasters

Visit the towns and villages clustered around the slopes of Vesuvius, on the eastern margins of the Bay of Naples, and you will find that a large number of local families own cats. This is partly out of affection for these friendly pets, of course, but there is an additional consideration that makes cats popular among people whose homes are built on the slopes of an active volcano.

Centuries of living with fiery death on the doorstep has taught them that when it comes to forecasting eruptions, there are few safer ways than to depend on a pet.

Just before volcanoes explode into life, cats, and some

other animals, frequently start to behave strangely, running frantically to and fro, complaining loudly, begging to be allowed out of the house and, once free, racing away from home to put as much distance as possible between themselves and areas threatened by lava flow. Their owners, if they've got any sense, are seldom too far behind them.

The story of Gianni and his black cat Toto is typical of many which I have heard in the volcano zones of Europe and the Far East.

It was late March 1944. After years of fighting, the war had finally come to an end with the arrival of Allied soldiers, allowing Gianni and his wife, Irma, to sleep peacefully in their farmhouse on the outskirts of the small town of San Sebastiano al Vesuvius.

Gianni's home, like the small town, lay in the track of a ravine along which, in the event of an eruption, lava could be expected to flow from a catchment area beneath the cone, the aptly named Valle dell'Inferno, to the plains below. Yet this fact had never disturbed the sixty-two-year-old farmer and his wife, nor especially concerned the inhabitants of San Sebastiano. The last major eruption, which had destroyed most of the town as well as the nearby village of Massa, had taken place eighty years earlier and nobody in the area believed that destruction on that scale was ever likely to occur again.

What Gianni and Irma did not, and could not, know was that even as they fell asleep on that chilly March night, Vesuvius was on the point of exploding into one of the longest, most violent and most destructive eruptions in recent history.

But Gianni's two-year-old cat, Toto, knew. Since the late afternoon of the previous day he had been restless, unwilling to eat and reluctant to remain indoors. Shortly after midnight on the morning of March 21 he awoke his master from a deep sleep by the effective, if painful, method of scratching his cheek.

Furious at the unprovoked attack, and still half asleep, the old man thrust Toto from him with a curse. But the cat refused to give up, returning to the attack again and again until his master jumped out of bed, bellowing with fury, and chased the animal around the room, threatening to skin him alive.

Finally Irma could stand it no longer and told her husband firmly to sit down and stop behaving so stupidly. Toto was a gentle, friendly creature and would never have attacked him without good reason. Deeply religious, the old woman regarded it as a sign from heaven for which there could only be one explanation—the volcano must be about to erupt.

Although Gianni protested angrily, complaining his wife was as mad as the cat, he finally agreed that they should dress, pack a few precious belongings into their hand-cart and walk through the darkness to her sister, who lived in an area normally safe from lava flow.

Within an hour of their departure, Vesuvius had erupted, and not long afterwards their home was crushed flat beneath the stream of incandescent lava which, pouring from the crater's rim in an eye-searing, half-mile-wide tidal wave of fire, swept on to engulf San Sebastiano al Vesuvius. Before its anger was exhausted, the volcano had killed nearly thirty people, twenty-one of them buried alive beneath a torrent of lava and cinders, destroyed the town and several villages and made more than 5,000 people homeless.

Gianni and Irma had been saved, and even managed to salvage their more precious possessions, thanks to the predictive powers of their faithful friend Toto, who fled to safety and was later reunited with them.

Cats are also skilled at forecasting earthquakes and here

too their sixth sense for danger can prove a good deal more reliable than the most elaborate electronic monitors.

In August 1979, for example, more than 200 instruments had been carefully positioned along the Calaveras Fault in California in order to detect the first signs of a quake, by no means a rare event in that part of the world. But these sophisticated pieces of technology were unable to predict a quake powerful enough to shake buildings 130 miles away in San Francisco. As a result the local people were unprepared, and there were injuries to people and damage to property.

This failure, though, can be contrasted with the strange succession of events which took place only three years earlier in the Friuli district of northeastern Italy, at the head of the Adriatic Sea.

On a quiet, cool, May evening, cats throughout the area suddenly began to behave very oddly indeed. They raced back and forth, scratched furiously at doors and windows and, once released, sped off into the darkness. At 9 P.M. the region was shaken by a major earthquake.

Such incidents have been repeated scores of times in those parts of the world where quakes are an ever-present hazard. Here, as in volcanic regions, local people place great faith in the predictive powers of their pets, especially cats, to warn them when danger is imminent.

So accurate are these forecasts, and so frequently have reliable reports of them been made during the past hundred years, that scientists around the world are now studying this phenomenon in the hope of harnessing the animal's unique abilities. The challenge facing researchers in the U.S., U.S.S.R., China and Germany—where the main studies are being carried out—is to discover exactly what it is that cats, and other creatures, are actually sensing. When the riddle is solved, scientists hope to construct mechanical devices to provide communities at risk with the same efficient early-warning system.

One investigator with a particular interest in the Friuli earthquake is Dr. Helmut Tributsch, a biochemist at the Max Planck Society's Fritz Haber Institute in Berlin. He was born in the Friuli region and has made a special study of how local animals behaved in the hours and minutes prior to the quake. Dr. Tributsch reports that all the cats in one village left their homes well before the shock waves struck, then stayed away for two days before venturing back. "In three cases, cats dragged kittens outdoors and bedded them in vegetation," he says.

According to American investigators, the same behavior occurred among California cats just before the 1979 earthquake. The U.S. Geological Survey, determined not to be caught unprepared a second time, has funded a massive research effort. Two of their scientists, Dr. Leon Otis, a clinical psychologist, and Dr. William Kautz, a computer specialist, are currently undertaking the largest-ever study of animal behavior as a predictor of forthcoming earthquakes. They have recruited and trained more than 10,000 volunteers who have instructions to keep a watchful eye on 200 species of animals and make detailed notes of everything they do. Observers are told to rate all behaviors on an "unusualness" scale of 1 to 4. If the animal in question ever does anything sufficiently peculiar to merit a score of 2 or more, the volunteers must immediately call the researchers on a permanently reserved hot line.

The vast quantity of data generated by this project is still being evaluated, but results so far strongly support folktales and popular belief about the ability of animals, and particularly cats, to forecast major natural catastrophes with astonishing reliability.

If you live in a danger zone, it really does appear that

keeping a watchful eye on your cat might, one day, save your life.

This has already happened in China where, in 1975, seismologists ordered the mass evacuation of Haicheng, a city in central China not far from the Great Wall, a full twenty-four hours before a major quake caused massive devastation to the area.

Western experts later learned that much of their predictive data had come from observing the behavior of animals. So impressed were the American scientists that a group of ten U.S. geologists and geophysicists visited China to find out more about the techniques involved.

According to Dr. Tributsch, the research so far suggests that the ability of cats to forecast earthquakes so efficiently is due to the fact that they are able to detect the presence of positively charged atoms (ions) in the surrounding atmosphere. These particles are released in huge numbers immediately prior to a quake, leaving the surrounding air almost alive with electrostatic activity.

Tributsch points out that the ancient Greeks and Romans occasionally reported strange portents, such as fog clouds or eerie lights in the heavens, immediately before a major quake, and such phenomena are due to increased electrical activity in the atmosphere.

Because we humans are fairly insensitive to such particles, even a massive increase of positive ions does little more than produce such minor reactions as a slight headache or increased irritability. But cats, being extremely responsive, suffer disturbances to both mood and behavior as the surrounding air triggers changes in the chemistry of their brains and nervous systems. One such change may be an increase in the production of serotonin, a chemical messenger which affects one's emotional state.

While there is good evidence to support the view that an

increase in ions does, indeed, influence the cat's behavior prior to eruptions or earthquakes, Dr. Ernst Kilian of Valdivia University in Chile, who has been gathering information about animals and earthquakes since 1960, has another explanation.

In his view cats can sense, and are upset by, the tiny tremors which precede major quakes. Since these are a far from uncommon phenomenon—thousands of minute tremors occur each year without leading to a major disaster—the prequake vibrations must be subtly different in some way. One possibility is that they possess a unique pattern which causes the cat, and other animals, to regard them as particularly menacing.

Dr. Kilian also believes that cats can sense magnetic phenomena imperceptible to humans. Changes in the surrounding magnetic field could be another early-warning signal of a major earthquake. (I shall be looking at other research into the detection of magnetic fields by cats in Chapter Seven and explaining how this may provide an answer to another, equally baffling, accomplishment.)

While sensitivity to positive ions, the patterns of tiny tremors and the ability to monitor changes in the earth's magnetic field may offer reasonable explanations for predictions of earthquake and volcanic eruptions, they provide no solution to the equally well-documented puzzle of how cats can foresee other types of accidents and disasters.

Two explanations seem likely. The first is that many events, including several of those I have described in this chapter, may involve sounds beyond the range of human hearing. The exploding television, for example, could well have been emitting ultra-high-frequency signals immediately before the tube blew. These would have irritated, and perhaps frightened, the sleeping cat, who left the room in protest.

On other occasions, cats may be picking up sounds whose frequency is too low for us to detect. Because our hearing fluctuates from one moment to the next, it is difficult to be specific about the upper and lower thresholds of human audition, whose peak sensitivity lies between 1,500 and 4,000 cycles per second (Hz), although much higher ranges can be heard if loud enough. By the age of fifty, the average person will require about a hundred times more power to hear a 5,000 Hz tone than he or she did at twenty. Animals possess a far more acute auditory sense. Mice, for instance, can pick up the squeaks of their companions at 100,000 Hz, and the cat's upper and lower limits are equally impressive.

In cats this ability, which has an important survival value, is combined with a facility for picking up very slight noises and distinguishing them against a background of other sounds. Riki, the ship's cat who saved the woman from drowning, probably detected her faint cries above the clamor of the vessel's engine and the surge of the waves. Human expressions of fear and distress are recognized as alarm calls both by cats and other pets.

But this very keen auditory sense is only part of the story, for cats also possess at least one additional and unique organ of detection. It is, literally, their sixth sense.

Called the vomeronasal organ, or organ of Jacobson, it consists of a small tube of cartilage, about half an inch long, located in the roof of the mouth and connected to the outside air by a small opening just behind the front teeth. Rudimentary traces of Jacobson's organ, named after a nineteenth-century Danish anatomist, are present in humans, but it no longer has any functional purpose.

In cats the organ forms part of the sense of smell and has nerves which take impulses directly to the olfactory regions of the brain. To use Jacobson's organ, the cat first has to stop whatever it is doing in order to suck air into the opening. This allows it to detect and identify various types of molecules floating around in the atmosphere. In this respect it is similar to the senses of taste and smell, but since they are already highly developed in the cat, and bearing in mind that nothing evolves in nature unless it has a specific purpose, Jacobson's organ must be performing some important additional sensory task.

You should be able to observe your own cat using this highly specialized organ by watching out for the following behavior. When about to draw air into the organ, the cat will suddenly stop dead still, half-open his mouth and pull back his lips, thus allowing as much air as possible to be drawn into the opening. I have observed this action many times and noticed that the sound as the air is sucked in may be heard quite clearly from several yards away. The cat's expression while performing this activity gives the impression of a grin or grimace. German animal experts refer to the behavior as the *flehmen* (grimace) response. It usually occurs when the cat is strolling through his territory, and may be accompanied by the raised foreleg and limp paw arousal signal, or some other indication of interest and alert attention.

We still do not know exactly what information the cat derives from Jacobson's organ, although it has been established that it plays a part in detecting sex-related pheromones in other cats. It is even possible that this sixth sense is at least partly responsible for some of the cat's remarkable predictions. If an event produced some tiny changes in the air's chemical composition, for example, as might happen prior to an eruption, earthquake, forest fire and so on, the ability to pick up and sample just a few molecules of matter might provide an early warning which no other animal could detect.

No theory, however, adequately accounts for the cat's extraordinary responsiveness to human need which has become so apparent from the stories in this and earlier chapters. Of course their extreme general sensitivity to the world around them must play an important part in this.

Here is an animal that can identify an owner's footfall from 100 yards away, notice the tiniest difference in voice tone or facial expression, hear sounds too high or too low for the human ear to discriminate, detect smells that pass unnoticed by ourselves and probably respond to features of the environment (such as changes in electrical charge, magnetic field or molecular composition) of which we remain entirely unaware.

But none of this is sufficient to persuade many cat-owners, and not a few scientific researchers, that cats do not possess supernatural as well as highly developed natural powers. For they believe that many of the more baffling predictions made by cats can only be explained by crediting them with some form of extrasensory perception.

CHAPTER 6

The Psychic Powers of Cats

So far we have explored aspects of the cat's incredible powers for which science can, in most cases, offer some sort of explanation, however incomplete and inadequate those theories may sometimes seem. But now, as we consider evidence for the psychic powers of cats, we shall be entering an area where many of the feats claimed cannot be explained in terms of current scientific knowledge and frequently appear to defy both reason and common sense. Indeed, researchers remain deeply divided over the most fundamental question of whether extrasensory perception—ESP as it is usually known—exists at all.

Let's start by defining exactly what is meant by the various terms used to describe psychic phenomena. ESP describes the ability to obtain knowledge or exert an influence over people, objects or events without employing direct physical means. Other frequently encountered expressions are *paranormal*, *parapsychological* and *parasensory*. The prefix *para*, taken from the Greek word meaning "beyond," indicates that science cannot, as yet, explain the mechanisms involved. Another frequently used expression is *psi*, first used by the pioneer ESP researcher Dr. Joseph Bank Rhine to describe any paranormal event. We shall be looking in some detail at the work of Dr. Rhine and his colleagues at Duke University both in this and the following chapter.

There are five major *psi* phenomena and all have been intensively studied by researchers in Europe, the United States and the Soviet Union:

Clairvoyance—the ability to obtain information about some inanimate object, such as an item of clothing, a purse, or watch, which is not apparent from its physical properties. For example, a clairvoyant, holding a man's tie, might gain the vivid impression of him injured and in a hospital with amnesia.

Psychokinesis—the movement of objects by non-physical means, as in poltergeist hauntings, which many consider extreme examples of this paranormal phenomenon.

Telepathy—the exchange of information between two or more minds by paranormal means.

Precognition—the ability to acquire knowledge about future events.

Spirit healing—as we have already seen, cats do have an astonishing healing ability, but my view is that this can be explained quite adequately without resorting to parapsychology.

So how many of the *psi* skills claimed to be present in

humans do cats possess? Dr. Rhine, who started the world's first laboratory for the investigation of parapsychology at Duke University, North Carolina, in the 1930s, has identified three psychic abilities that he believes can be found in many cats.

The first, a reaction to impending danger either to itself or its owner (precognition), we examined in the previous chapter. The second, a form of telepathy, is the ability to respond to the death or distress of their owners over a long distance. Finally, cats appear to anticipate, with uncanny accuracy, the return of their owners after a long absence, another example of precognition. Other research findings, which I shall be looking at later on, and a massive amount of anecdotal evidence point to their ability to use both psychokinesis and clairvoyance as well.

Although the whole area of study is highly controversial, the existence of psychic powers in cats, and some other animals, finds support among several eminent scientists, including one of the world's most respected ethnologists, the Dutch Nobel prize–winner Nikko Tinbergen, who writes: "If one applies the term [ESP] to perception by processes not yet known to us, the extrasensory perception among living creatures may well occur widely."

This view is supported by Dr. Robert Morris, research coodinator of the Physical Research Foundation in Durham, North Carolina. "The use of animals in parapsychology is just beginning," he says. One of Dr. Morris's favorite research animals is the cat, and I will be describing some of his experiments later in this chapter.

Over the last ten years I have followed up scores of cat ESP stories and examined details of hundreds of other tales which have been published in newspapers and magazines around the world. Although there are many accounts on record of extrasensory powers being displayed by horses and dogs, the sheer number and uniqueness of those in which cats play a principal part strongly suggest that they, more than any other animals, may possess very special psychic ability.

It must, of course, be remembered that anecdotes are a very poor foundation on which to try to construct any sort of scientific theory. People's perceptions of events are known to be distorted by a whole range of preconceptions and prejudices, many of which they may be quite unaware of. Even the most honest and reliable of witnesses make mistakes, misinterpret information, are swayed in their judgments by the opinions or convictions of others. Many fabricate or exaggerate tales for a whole variety of reasons, including a desire for attention, to perpetuate a good hoax on researchers and the gullible and even in the hope of earning some easy money by selling their fantasies to the press!

All I can claim about the case histories described here is that they do seem to suggest that, on some occasions and under certain circumstances, cats can exhibit abilities that defy rational explanation.

The first story, if correctly reported, reveals the parasensory powers of precognition and, perhaps, telepathy.

The Cat That Came to Mourn

In the whole south-coast resort of Bournemouth, England, there could have been few closer friends than sixty-three-year-old Martin and his cat Fidget, aged six. They had been together ever since the stray had been given a home by the ex-policeman.

One morning Martin set off to have lunch with a friend in Southampton. As he only expected to be away for a few hours, Fidget was locked up in the house with sufficient food and water to last him through the day. But as Martin made his way home, he was knocked down by a bus and critically injured. Rushed to hospital, he lay in intensive care for three days. His last thoughts were for Fidget and the authorities arranged for a kindly neighbor to take care of him. Finally Martin sank into a deep coma and died without regaining consciousness. Two days afterward he was buried in a large, bleak cemetery near his home. When Martin's friend arrived to attend the burial service he expected to mourn alone. But he was wrong, for Fidget had already arrived, soon after dawn according to one of the groundsmen, and was waiting patiently beside the open grave to bid his master farewell.

The cat stayed, motionless as a statue, until the coffin was lowered into the earth, when he turned and walked dejectedly away. Martin's friend, who recounted this strange story to me, has no doubt in his mind that the cat really was Fidget.

"He had such distinctive markings I would have recognized him anywhere," he said. "Amazing as it may seem, he somehow knew not only that his pal was dead but exactly when and where in that large graveyard he was going to be buried."

This ability to sense the death of a beloved human has been recounted in several stories about feline ESP.

In his book *The Psychic Powers of Animals*, author Bill Schul describes how, after Richard H. Lee of Prescott, Arizona, had been killed in a car accident, his devoted black tomcat started behaving very strangely. The crash occurred shortly before midnight and, soon after, the distraught Mrs. Lee noticed that the cat was racing back and forth on the front lawn in a highly excited manner. He refused to enter the house or allow his mistress to touch him. "When I took out some food, he climbed the stone wall at the back of the house in a perfect panic,'' she recalled. The cat never did return home, but hung around the neighborhood for months afterward, occasionally returning to stare intently at the house for hours on end.

Perhaps the cat was watching out for his master's ghost, because there are a host of tales—and even some research evidence—which suggest that cats are able to see into the realm of spirits.

The Cat and the Haunted Helm

Long voyages during which one is constantly at the mercy of the elements inevitably make sailors more superstitious than most, and there are few mariners who can't tell you some supernatural sea story.

Fatigue, danger and periods of isolation on a long sea voyage all add to the psychological stresses and make the human mind especially susceptible to illusion and delusion. However, extremely strange and well-authenticated incidents *have* happened on ocean voyages. This story of the cat and the haunted helm is certainly one of the strangest.

It was told to me by an old seaman as we sat together in the shade of a public park above the Grand Harbor of Valletta in Malta. Below us, and beyond the busy dockyard, the blue Mediterranean looked peaceful and welcoming, but the man was soon recalling less tranquil seas when he had been the mate aboard a Panamanian-registered, Greek-owned, rust-bucket of a cargo vessel with a French captain and a largely Asian crew.

They were homeward bound from Melbourne, and had made good time toward the Cape, when the elderly ship's overtaxed main engine finally gave up and they drifted in high seas while the cursing engineers did their best to patch up the damage so that the vessel could limp into Cape Town.

The captain drank heavily and drove his crew hard, especially the second mate, a German called Hansen, against whom he appeared to nurse a deep personal hatred. None of the other sailors ever understood the cause of his spite, since the man, a shy, unsociable individual in his late thirties, worked hard and did his job efficiently.

"Hansen's only friend aboard was Rhaj, the ship's cat," the sailor told me. "And he was the only person who liked the cat, which was a scruffy, spiteful animal. The German fed the cat, allowed it to sleep on his bunk and talked to it for hours on end." It would follow him like a dog wherever he went in the ship.

The engine breakdown made the captain even more shorttempered than usual and most of his anger was vented on the unfortunate second mate. One night he arrived on the bridge well the worse for drink and began to abuse the helmsman for not doing his job properly. The second mate protested and the captain struck him in the face, sending the man spinning against a steel bulkhead. His head struck an angle of metal with savage force, which cracked his skull, killing him instantly.

He was buried at sea the following day. That evening, when the watch changed, the ship's cat appeared on the bridge and stayed staring impassively toward the spot where his friend used to stand on duty. When the time came for the mate to go below, the cat rose and pattered silently away. His strange behavior quickly attracted the attention of the crew, for according to them, the pattern of his behavior exactly followed the dead man's daily routine.

He woke at the same time and walked to the washroom and heads, then proceeded to the saloon before making his rounds of the vessel. Before long the seamen concluded that the cat wasn't merely acting out the second mate's daily schedule of activities, he was actually following the ghost of his friend around the vessel. As the rumors spread, the crew, already unnerved by the second mate's violent death, became even more unsettled. Soon the whole ship was filled with dark forebodings.

The captain, who by now seemed to spend more time drunk than sober, ordered his officers to catch the cat and toss him over the side in the hope of calming his sailors down. But no sooner had the order been given than Rhaj vanished from sight. The next time he was seen, two days later, he was curled contentedly on the dead captain's face.

The man had apparently collapsed onto his bunk while drunk and fallen asleep. Somehow Rhaj had managed to get into the cabin and curl up over the man's mouth and nose, very effectively suffocating him. When the ship docked, the cat walked quietly down the gangway and was never seen again.

"The strange thing was the lock," the seaman who recounted this tale to me concluded. "The captain always locked his cabin door from the inside. It was like that when we found it. They had to break the door open to get in. There *was* a spare key—the skipper kept it in a drawer of his chart table on the bridge. Not many of the crew knew it was there—he liked to have his little secrets, did the old man. But there was one person who, to my certain knowledge, knew exactly where the key was kept. That was the dead second mate, Hansen."

If cats can see human ghosts, there is no reason why they should not also be able to observe the spirits of dead animals, and those who have investigated the psychic powers of cats, like author Bill Schul, came across many stories which suggest that they can.

The Ghost Cat on the Cushion

After the death of her beloved cat Fingal, his owner, Celia Dale, used to be disturbed by a soft tapping noise at the French windows. This always occurred around 9 P.M., the time when Fingal would beg to be let in again after his evening exercise.

One afternoon a family friend brought her Siamese on a visit. The animal started walking toward the armchair where Fingal always slept on a special yellow cushion. Suddenly the cat froze, arched her back and started spitting in rage. According to the women, her behavior was exactly as if she had spotted another cat asleep on the chair.

A short while later, at about the time that Fingal had always been allowed out, Celia Dale happened to open the French windows. Immediately the Siamese, who had previously avoided the armchair, rose to her feet, quickly crossed the room and curled herself contentedly on the cushion. It was exactly as if she had seen the other cat disappear and knew that it was finally safe to curl up on the armchair.

While discussing ghosts, we should also explore the possibility that humans can see the forms of departed animals as well as the spirits of humans, since these encounters have frequently been described.

The Ghost of the Congleton Cat

Soon after the turn of the century, a certain Englishwoman, Louise Marlowe, was visiting a friend who lived in the Cheshire market town of Congleton. One afternoon they set off by pony and trap to explore the remains of an ancient abbey. While walking toward the ruins, the women noticed a large white cat sitting on a post and debated whether the beautiful animal would allow them to pet it.

As they approached, however, the cat suddenly jumped into the air and disappeared. The surrounding countryside was flat and lacked any sort of hiding place, which made the animal's vanishing act all the more perplexing. After searching and calling without success for a few moments, the two women abandoned the hunt and turned their attention to the ruins.

A few days later, when driving past the same spot, they again noticed the cat perched on the same post. The animal watched them in a friendly way but, as on the previous occasion, disappeared while they were walking toward it.

Later that afternoon they stopped for tea at a small café and told the elderly waitress of their strange encounters.

"You drove by at just the right time to see Congleton's ghost cat," she told them.

The old woman, who had lived in the area for more than fifty years, explained that she could remember the cat when it was alive, the devoted pet of a Mrs. Winge, housekeeper at the abbey. One day the cat did not return home and Mrs. Winge feared he had been killed by a pack of dogs known to be roaming the area. That evening, however, she heard a familiar scratching at the back door and, opening it, was delighted to see the cat sitting placidly on her step. But no matter how much she coaxed and pleaded, the animal refused to come indoors. Then, after a few moments, he slowly vanished before her astonished gaze. Following that first visitation, the animal reappeared night after night and was seen not only by the housekeeper but by friends and visitors.

This story has one intriguing literary footnote that came to light during my own investigations. The manner in which the Congleton ghost is said to have slowly disappeared reminds one of fiction's best-known disappearing trick, that performed by the Cheshire Cat in *Alice's Adventures in Wonderland*.

According to Louis Carroll, this creature "vanished quite slowly, beginning with the end of the tail, and ending with the grin, which remained for some time after the rest of it had gone."

Could Congleton's ghost have been the inspiration for Carroll's Cheshire Cat? There is certainly circumstantial evidence to support such an idea. The dates are about right—Alice's adventures were first published in 1865—and so is the location. Louis Carroll, or Charles Lutwidge Dodgson to give him his correct name, was born at Daresbury in Cheshire, which is not all that far from Congleton, so he might well have learned of the ghost. Finally, such a strange and mystical story would surely have appealed to the imagination of this shy Oxford mathematician, whose interest in the paranormal was such that he joined the Society for Psychical Research very shortly after its formation in 1882.

The next story, from India, seems to suggest that some cats possess the *psi* powers of both precognition and clairvoyance.

The Cat Who Was in at the Kill

Peggy Pease was one of those indomitable colonial ladies who have outlived their time. She had come to India as a governess before the First World War, married a veterinary surgeon in the army and become a pillar of her local society. The years passed, the world she knew changed beyond recognition, but Peggy stayed on in the only country she really knew. On his retirement, her husband and she opened a small animal hospital, where they dispensed skill and tenderness to any creature in distress.

After his death, she carried on the work until, well into her seventies, ill-health obliged her to close down the sanctuary. However, she continued to look after any strays who came her way, and these included several cats, the most magnificent of them being a tabby called Poona.

After spending much of her life waited on by a house full of servants, the old lady was now attended by just three, a young boy, a cook who was almost as elderly as herself, and a middle-aged man who had entered her service only a few months earlier. Friends had warned Peggy he was not to be trusted but, strong-willed as ever, she claimed to be an excellent judge of character. As things turned out, it was to prove a fatal mistake. Because she seldom left home, nobody noticed her absence for several days. Only when two friends called on her by chance and found the house was deserted was it realized that she and her servants had vanished.

The police were called and the place searched without success. Then the detectives, hearing a frantic meowing coming from a store cupboard, unlocked the door to find Poona and three of her companions in a desperate condition. Two of the animals were so weak from lack of food and water that nothing could be done to save them, but the others soon recovered their strength.

A couple of days later, Poona turned up at the local police station, was recognized by the officer in charge and taken back to the friend who was caring for Peggy's pets. But, every day from then on, Poona made his way straight to the police station and started making a fuss at the officer on duty.

Nearly a week went by, with no sign of either the old woman or her servants, before one of the detectives had a crazy hunch. Taking Poona back to his mistress's home, the officer presented the cat with an item of Peggy's clothing. His idea was simply that if dogs could follow a scent, why couldn't one use a cat in the same way? He was quickly to discover that Poona possessed tracking skills which would put even the most successful bloodhound to shame.

For several moments the cat made no move. Then he slowly sank on his haunches and stared, ears twitching and tail flicking the air urgently, toward a thick clump of undergrowth flanking a small river at the bottom of the garden. Rising again, he strolled purposefully toward one particular patch of tangled vegetation close to the water's edge and sat down again. Excited, but still not sure his bright idea had paid off, the policeman searched the bushes and was quickly rewarded by the discovery of a wooden mallet heavily stained with blood and hair.

But Poona's revelations were far from finished. With what looked like a murder weapon located, he turned his gaze toward the house. Once again he made no move for some time until, seemingly satisfied, he went unhesitatingly toward a flower bed and started scratching vigorously at the earth. The detective sent for help and before long the bed was being dug up. The killer had done a thorough burial job after murdering the old lady and her cook. They shared a grave more than six feet deep.

The remaining adult servant was arrested a week later but, at first, protested his innocence. He claimed to have been away visiting a brother the morning his mistress had disappeared and found the house deserted on his return. He also had a confident explanation as to how his fingerprints came to be on the mallet. It was a tool he frequently used to do odd jobs around the house, he told the detectives calmly.

But then Poona was brought into the room and immediately flew for the man's face, spitting and clawing until he was pulled off. When the detectives explained how the cat had found both murder weapon and victims, the servant's nerve suddenly snapped and he confessed the whole sordid crime. Having been caught stealing by Peggy, he had been dismissed. Later that afternoon, he returned to the house and bludgeoned her to death, killing the cook and the boy to eliminate any witnesses. Two of the corpses he buried; the boy's body he had flung into a river.

"No one saw what I had done except the cats," the man said fearfully. But even they did not witness the burial of the bodies or hiding of the murder weapon, since the murderer had shut them all in the windowless store cupboard immediately after the slaying. It was his realization that the cat could only have discovered both his victims and the weapon used to kill them by occult powers that terrified the murderer into confessing his crime.

Mystical Cats

While all the stories I have described sound so fantastic to modern ears that many will be inclined either to dismiss them as absurd or seek to explain them in some more rational manner, people in earlier times would have accepted them without question. Indeed, such tales of the supernatural would have done no more than confirm them in an already well-established belief that the cat was a familiar of witches, an instrument of sorcery, an adept in the black arts and the embodiment of all evil.

This superstition may well have had its earliest roots in Greek mythology, for according to classical legend, Galinthia, daughter of Proetus, King of Thebes, was transformed into a cat by the angry Fates and condemned to dwell in Hades.

The myth tells how Alcmene, a friend of Galinthia, was about to give birth to Hercules. Jealous of her labor, the Fates worked magical charms in an attempt to prevent the child's birth. To distract them from their spells, Galinthia falsely announced that the child had already been born.

So startled were the hostile goddesses by her unexpected news that they momentarily released one another's hands, thus breaking the charm and allowing Hercules to be born. To revenge themselves, the Fates turned Galinthia into a cat—condemning her, they hoped, to wander the world as an outcast for all time. But Hecate, the Queen of Hell, who taught sorcery and witchcraft, took pity on her and made the cat into the high priestess in her kingdom of the dead and damned.

The association between cats and the black arts goes back centuries, one of the earliest links being with the Cathars, a religious sect that dominated many parts of Europe during the twelfth century.

Cathars believed that the God of the Old Testament was Satan, who, having created the world, now controlled all human destiny. They regarded procreation as a sin, since this only served to populate the Devil's world, and some lived in great austerity, refraining from sex, violence, the eating of any food derived from animals, the ownership of property, taking oaths and telling lies.

Other Cathars, however took the more pragmatic view that since they were already damned and in bondage to Satan, nothing they could do would make matters worse, so they enjoyed lives of unrestrained debauchery.

Cathars regarded themselves as representing the true Church of Christ, considered the Church of Rome an instrument of the Devil, and denounced the Pope as anti-Christ. Not surprisingly, perhaps, the Catholic Church took grave exception to such heretical views, and during the thirteenth century Pope Innocent III dispatched an armed crusade against Cathars in southern France. Thousands were slaughtered in battle or captured to suffer torture and execution.

In their agony at the hands of their inquisitors, Cathars confessed to flying through the air to their meetings on broomsticks, slaughtering stolen children, drinking potions made from human flesh and worshipping Satan in the form of a cat—exactly the same charges which the church would later make against witches.

The Luciferans, self-admitted Satanists whose sect flourished in Germany during the early thirteenth century, regarded the cat as a symbol of their master, the Prince of Darkness. At the start of their ceremonies, which involved feasting and sexual orgies, a large black cat would emerge from a secret compartment in a grotesque statue of Satan and move among the worshippers. Those considered worthy of the ultimate honor were then allowed to kiss the animal's bottom.

But it is a mistake to think that the ancient link between cats and sorcery ended centuries ago. As recently as 1942 a cat was boiled alive during a grisly Satanic ritual attended by naked men and women in the Spanish Basque country, while only a couple of years ago I learned of a group of devil worshippers in New York whose bizarre acts of sacrilege included the worship of black cats.

Other animals, it is true, were sometimes named as familiars during witchcraft trials, including toads, snakes, rats, dogs and goats. But cats, more than any other living creature, seem to have symbolized sorcery for the better part of a thousand years. Even today, black cats are held in superstitious awe by many, being regarded as signs of good omen in Britain and portents of ill-fortune in the U.S.

Were cats chosen by mystics because they were so aloof

and readily available or because they also possessed psychic powers? If so, could their *psi* skills ever be tested under laboratory conditions?

Dr. Robert Morris of North Carolina is one of the number of researchers in different parts of the world who has spent years trying to do just that. He describes one informal but intriguing study in which a cat was taken into an allegedly haunted house which had two especially sinister rooms where murders had been committed. When placed in these rooms, the cat immediately protested loudly and appeared extremely frightened. Taken into any of the other rooms, however, she remained calm and showed no distress.

Given the cat's sensitivity to temperatures, it is interesting to note that when humans went into the supposedly "haunted" rooms they all reported feeling chilly and insisted that the temperature must have suddenly fallen. One person estimated the drop as being at least 20°F. A thermometer registered no change at all.

Dr. Morris and his colleagues at the Physical Research Foundation are using cats in studies of out-of-the-body, or *ecsomatic*, experiences—those occasions when people suddenly find themselves observing all that is happening from the viewpoint of an onlooker. A typical example, reported by Celia Green, Director of the Institute of Psychophysical Research at Oxford, in her book *Out-of-the-Body Experiences*, concerns a feverish hospital patient who suddenly became aware of being "no longer in my body but up in the corner of my cubicle watching the nurses flitting about . . . bathing the body lying in my bed, etc." Not only could this person see what was going on, she could also hear everything that was said between the nurses and doctors. This bizarre experience lasted eight or nine days, during which the patient explains: "I felt no pain, but I sometimes wanted to tell one of the nurses something but

could never make her hear.'' Finally her temperature returned to normal and she found herself reunited with her
body.

In Dr. Morris's study, one cat in particular, the pet of a
subject who claimed to make frequent ecsomatic trips, became extremely placid and relaxed at precisely those times
when her owner claimed to be visiting her during an out-
of-the-body expedition. At all other times the cat behaved
in a perfectly normal, active and energetic fashion. None
of those observing the animal had any idea when the subject claimed to be making her trips away from the physical
body and so could not have been providing the cats with
clues, consciously or unconsciously.

Two other researchers, Drs. Karlis Ossi and Esther Foster, examined the ability of kittens to detect which of two
arms in a maze held food by using only ESP. The kittens
were first trained to expect that food might be placed at the
end of either arm of the maze. Fans were used to blow air
toward the food, so carrying its scent away from the kittens
and preventing them from homing in using their keen sense
of smell.

If the kittens chose the arm of the maze containing the
food more often than the empty arm it could be argued that
some form of ESP allowed them to make this above-chance
prediction of the right route to take. Under good conditions, that is when they were content, affectionately treated
and not distracted from the task, it was shown that kittens
did indeed enter the correct arm significantly more often
than they went into the empty arm.

If they were made to run the maze under "bad" conditions, that is, after rough handling or while being distracted, their number of misses was, again, considerably
higher than would be expected by chance. The kittens also
did poorly whenever their responses took on a stereotyped

character, that is, if they always went either to the left or the right, or switched from left to right arm and back again consistently.

The strongest indications that paranormal powers were working for them in a positive and helpful manner, therefore, came when the cats were at ease, felt secure and could focus all their attention on the task in a relieved, flexible manner. ESP seemed to have a more negative effect on those occasions when the kittens were stressed, distracted or got into unhelpful and rigid response patterns. As any researcher into human ESP will confirm, these are exactly the same conditions under which human subjects seem to produce their best, and worst, results during all kinds of parapsychology experiments.

Studies have also been carried out to see if cats possess any psychokinetic powers. In one investigation a cat was placed in a special cage designed so that some important aspect of his environment, such as the temperature or lighting, was regulated by a device outside the cage which automatically and randomly changed the conditions, for example by suddenly decreasing the heat or switching on a light. The question being posed was whether cats would be able to influence the functioning of this mechanical regulator, so as to enjoy the most comfortable surroundings, purely by an effort of will. The answer appears to be that, at least to some extent, this is exactly what cats do. When it was cold, for instance, the regulator kept the heater on for longer periods and more frequently than could have been expected by chance.

Left Brain vs Right Brain

An interesting aspect of feline ESP is that of dominance by either the left or right side of the brain. As most people know, the mammalian brain comprises two hemispheres linked together by a thick band of connective tissue. The left brain, which controls movement on the right side of the body, is primarily concerned with logical reasoning, deductive problem-solving and such complex intellectual tasks as numerical calculations. In most people, especially those who are right-handed, the language centers, which enable us to speak and understand the spoken word, are located in this hemisphere.

The right side of the brain deals with more intuitive, imaginative and less logical mental processes. It is the portion of the brain where we dream our dreams, come up with hunches, indulge in fantasies and engage in creative thinking.

This suggests that left-handed people, in whom the right side of the brain will be dominant, should be less logical and more intuitive, less calculating and more creative, less materialistic and more mystical in their thoughts than right-handed, left-brain-dominated individuals.

Interestingly, the word *sinister* comes from the Latin meaning "left" and can mean, according to the Oxford English Dictionary: "Portending or indicating misfortunes or disaster." In magic, taking the left-hand path means following the devil and practising the black arts rather than using such powers for good. Could it be that these beliefs first arose because left-handed people tended to possess greater paranormal powers than the less imaginative, down-to-earth right-handers?

Some researchers believe that this might well have influenced people in their decision to dabble in the occult and, later, their successes may have led them to be highly regarded as practitioners of sorcery and witchcraft. It is here, then, that we find a fascinating link with current research into the "handedness" of cats.

Studies by Dr. J. Cole of the Laboratory of Physiology at Oxford University have revealed that a majority of cats favor their left paw, either consistently or very frequently. After testing 60 cats, he found that 35 had a marked left-paw preference, with 23 of these being exclusively left-pawed.

Dr. Cole concluded that handedness definitely exists among cats but that, unlike humans, most favor the left side, so indicating right-brain domination.

If you are interested in testing your own cat, you can easily do so using the same technique that Dr. Cole employed in his laboratory. All you need is a sheet of stiff cellophane, which should be rolled into a tube about three inches wide and fastened by tape onto a piece of stiff card. Place the device on the floor and let your cat become familiar with it before you proceed. Now give your cat a scrap of his favorite food. When this has been eaten, place a second tidbit just in front of the mouth of the tube so that he can easily pick it up. Now for the real test. Place the food inside the tube and watch which paw the cat uses to retrieve it. Repeat this test ten times and notice whether either paw is favored. If it is, and if that paw is the left one, then the chances are good that your cat has above-average powers of ESP. (In Chapter Nine I will be describing some ways in which you can put your cat's psychic powers to the test, as well as telling you how to assess your pet on other skills.)

There is one other activity in which cats frequently reveal an ability which appears to depend on some form of paranormal powers. That is on those far from infrequent occasions when a cat travels hundreds or even thousands of miles across unfamiliar territory to be reunited with its owner.

CHAPTER 7

Incredible Journeys

Pitchou, the kitten, didn't have much of a trail to follow. All he knew was that his master, Fernand Schmitt, had gone away on a train. But that was the only clue he needed to complete a journey of more than seventy-five miles through the Vosges mountains in France. Eleven days after setting off from home, Pitchou crawled, bedraggled, hungry and exhausted, into the army barracks where twenty-year-old Fernand was sleeping.

The kitten's adventures were pieced together from the evidence of railway workers who had noticed him plodding wearily along the tracks, army officers who observed his unexpected arrival at the Strasbourg military barracks, and the vet who treated him for a bad case of sore paws.

The saga began when Fernand left his home in Merlebach to join the army. Pitchou was taken to the station to see the young man off and watched as the train carried him out of sight. The next day he vanished from home.

127

"By some extraordinary sense of smell, the kitten was able to follow the track," said the army vet in his official report of the incident. "He went through tunnels, stations and across bridges. His instinct was perfect."

But Pitchou's achievement, while considerable, is by no means the longest, the most hazardous or the most remarkable trip ever made by a cat. Even Sugar's accomplishment in trailing her mistress half across the United States is by no means the greatest epic in the annals of incredible cat journeys.

The American speed record for a reunion between cat and owner was set in 1949 by Rusty, who followed his owner from Boston, Massachusetts, to Chicago, Illinois, a distance of some 950 miles covered in 83 days, or at well over 10 miles per day. To keep up such a cracking pace Rusty must, of course, have hitched lifts in passing trucks and railroad cars.

The British record is held by a three-year-old Tabby named McCavity, who walked 500 miles from his new home in Cumbernauld to his old home near Truro, in Cornwall, in only three weeks.

Stories like this support the view of scientists who report that, apart from pigeons, cats have navigational powers far superior to any in the animal kingdom.

There are, in fact, two kinds of homing journey made by cats. Type I homing occurs after a pet has been stolen, given away to another owner, moves with the family to a new house or gets lost a long way from home. Here the challenge is to return to a familiar base after starting out in unfamiliar surroundings. Although this may sound like an impossible task, cats frequently manage it with apparent ease and in a very short space of time.

Even more baffling, however, is Type II homing, which

happens after an animal is left behind when an owner moves to a different address and somehow tracks down the owner.

The distances involved in both types of homing have ranged from just a few miles to many thousands. Shorter trips typically take from a few days to several weeks, while the longer journeys may last months or even years. At the end of the trail, the cat usually manages to arrive, often in a state of great exhaustion, either at precisely the right address or very close to it.

Before we look at the ways in which scientists are investigating such homing abilities and seeking rational explanations for what sometimes seem almost supernatural accomplishments, let's consider two more cases in which cats traveled vast distances to be reunited with their owners.

The first is an excellent example of Type I homing.

The Cat Who Came Home from Wales

Margaret Adams had given up all hope of ever seeing her cat, Sampson, again after he disappeared during a caravan vacation in Wales, over 250 miles from his east London home. She placed advertisements in local newspapers and notified the police stations over a wide area without success. Sadly she accepted that her much-loved pet would never return.

It was two years before Sampson came back into her life. Going into the garden of her Plaistow home to bring in her weekly washing from the line, she saw a travel-weary animal perched on the wall. Then she noticed that he had the same white patch of fur at the base of his stomach and the same short, fat legs as her long-lost pet. Hardly daring to believe her eyes, Margaret called his name and the cat responded immediately. Sampson had finally come home from Wales.

The second story involves a Type II homing and concerns a cat who discovered her owner's new address after an absence of almost three years.

The Cat Who Was Stolen Away

Nobody who saw Cindy could fail to be impressed. An elegant red tabby, she excited admiration and comment from every cat-lover she met, and that's how her troubles began.

One July her owner, Brenda James, took Cindy on a visit to her brother, who lived on the outskirts of Manchester, England. One evening they went to the theater and returned to find the house burgled. Stolen property included silver ornaments, a portable TV, some cash—and Cindy. She had been "catnapped" by a thief who had obviously found her enchanting appearance too much of a temptation.

Every effort was made to trace the stolen animal, but without success, and a heartbroken Brenda traveled home alone. About eighteen months after the theft, she moved from her house in west London to a new address some three miles away.

Ten months later, returning home after a weekend away, she found a note from the woman next door. It reported finding a half-starved cat sitting on Brenda's doormat late on Saturday afternoon. It had been meowing so pathetically that she had taken it in. She wondered if the animal might belong to Brenda.

Amazingly, it did. Five minutes later a delighted and bewildered Brenda had been reunited with her pet. Not only had Cindy made the long journey down from the north of England to west London, but she had somehow managed to discover her mistress's new address.

A major objection to such stories is, of course, that of identification. How can one ever be certain that the animal claimed as the missing pet is not simply a stray with similar markings?

This possibility was carefully guarded against in one of the most detailed scientific investigations of incredible journeys conducted at Duke University by Drs. Joseph Rhine and Sara Feather. They searched newspaper and magazine files, requested assistance from friends and publicized their desire for any information about animals making long trips home. Of the hundreds of stories which came to their attention, only fifty-two passed their stringent acceptance criteria as deserving further examination. To qualify for investigation, each account had to meet four requirements.

First, it had to come from a reliable source, that is, the owners themselves rather than friends or relatives. Second, the animal had to possess some distinctive feature, a scar, unique markings, some physical deformity—as in the case of Sugar's left hip—which would guarantee accurate identification. There had to be corroboration, in the form of eyewitness testimony from independent witnesses, and finally the animal itself had to be alive for examination.

A typical story from their final selection concerns the homing powers of a solid white, half-Persian, four-year-old male called Beau Chat. He belonged to a family living in Lafayette, Louisiana, but was the special pet of their eight-year-old son Butchie.

One day in the winter of 1953 they visited Texarkana, 294 miles away, to look for a house. In their absence, Beau Chat vanished from home and could not be found. The husband remained in Texarkana and, in January 1954, was joined by his wife and two children. About four months later the cat suddenly turned up at the school where the wife was a teacher and the boy a student.

"They first heard about him from other children, who said he ran from them," says Dr. Rhine. "But when Butchie saw the cat, he walked right up to him, picked him up, and said immediately, 'It's Beau Chat.' "

An unusual feature of this cat's upbringing was that he had been raised by the family's collie, along with her pups, and had learned to growl like a dog and bite when angry. He also answered to a whistle. All these responses were present in the newly arrived cat, who was immediately recognized not only by the family but also by their collie. The dog had always allowed Beau Chat to sleep beside her, a courtesy she instantly extended to the visitor. Further confirmation of identity came from two exceptional physical characteristics: a scar over one eye, which prevented it from completely closing, and a smear of tar on the tail. This mark, acquired in Louisiana, had never been completely removed. There was also a nick in the cat's ear which exactly matched one sustained by Beau Chat, although Dr. Rhine attaches less importance to this feature, since nicks in the ears of a tomcat are not all that distinctive. Finally, there was the cat's state on arrival at the school and the fact that, out of all the children, he allowed only Butchie to approach and pick him up.

With twenty-two well-documented reports of cat journeys on file, Drs. Rhine and Feather expressed themselves completely satisfied that trips over distances of up to 3,000 miles were a genuine phenomenon and not the result of coincidence and self-delusion.

This belief is shared by biologist Dr. Roger Tabor, who has made a special study of cats who have reverted back to the wild. "A pet cat treats the family with whom it stays

as a substitute for a group of cats, and it will tend to return
to them as well as to its familiar surroundings,'' he explains. ''I know of many well-authenticated cases of cats
returning home . . . which shows that they have navigational ability.''

These views are supported by the evidence of experiments in which the cat's homing skills have been put to
the test under carefully controlled conditions. In one of the
earliest studies, carried out in 1921 in Cleveland, Ohio,
Professor Frank Herrick investigated cats' navigational
skills by the simple expedient of driving his own pet five
miles from home and then releasing him in the unfamiliar
countryside.

After the shock of this unexpected treachery had passed,
the cat immediately turned in the correct direction for home
and set off at a brisk pace, followed by the Professor, who
struggled to keep up as his pet ran across fields, bounded
over walls, wriggled through hedges and sped nimbly along
woodland tracks. Finally, with the scientist a good deal
more exhausted than the cat, they arrived safely home. Not
only had the cat accomplished the journey without hesitation, he had also found the shortest return route.

When he had recovered both his breath and his astonish-
ment at this achievement, Professor Herrick decided to see
whether the same remarkable navigational skills could be
found in cats other than his own. Collecting a group of
animals from friends and neighbors, he abandoned them at
varying distances to discover how far their homing instinct
would hold true. He found that every cat was able to orient
itself in the unfamiliar surroundings with little effort and
then set off in the correct direction. To prevent the cats
creating a mental map as they were transported to the starting point, Herrick doped them so that they slept soundly

for the entire journey. But even this made absolutely no difference to their ability to head straight for home.

As a result of these experiments, Herrick concluded that cats possess what he terms a "direction constant," a navigational sense which does not rely on remembering details of an outward trip.

A similar research approach was taken by Drs. H. Precht and E. Lindenbaum of Germany's Kiel University, who wanted to discover how cats worked out which direction to take as they started out for home. They transported cats, in closed boxes to prevent them seeing where they were going, to a variety of test sites located at different distances from their owners' houses. On arrival, the cats were placed inside a maze which had twenty-four different exits and allowed to escape. In a significant number of instances, the cats chose to leave the maze through an opening which faced the direction in which their home lay.

A similar study was conducted by Dr. B. Grzimek, who used pigeons as well as cats and a maze with only three exits. His findings confirmed the Kiel research, and added the surprising detail that in this test cats proved superior to pigeons. It is important to bear in mind that the maze experiment only measures the initial orientation response and in a genuine contest the bird still proves superior to the cat.

This homing instinct can be found very early on in the cat's life, although it is much less developed in kittens than mature adults. Dr. Jay Rosenblatt and his colleagues at the Institute of Animal Behavior at Rutgers University, in Newark, New Jersey, found that a small "home region," the area where they spend most of their time, develops as an orientation center—a kind of homing beacon—during the first three weeks of life.

The kitten's attachment to the "home region" is based not on sight, which is just starting to develop, but on scent.

The area is staked out with pheromone markers deposited both by themselves and by their mother, and confinement to this area ensures that the young animals never stray too far from Mom's watchful gaze. Kittens are observed to be calmer while in the "home" area and visual orientation appears earlier in this region.

As cats mature, this smell-homing ability becomes increasingly powerful and is believed to play a major part in enabling them to travel swiftly and confidently around familiar territory. Fully grown cats are often observed placing copious amounts of their personal scent on important landmarks, sometimes referred to as "odor sticks" by the experts. It is possible, therefore, that as the cat ranges its "home" area, which may cover many square miles, it puts down chemical trails with which to navigate itself home.

While there is, at present, no scientific confirmation that such scent routes exist, they could provide part of the explanation of Type I homing, where a cat lost in an unfamiliar territory makes its way unerringly home. It may be that tiny amounts of scent, wafted by the breeze and possibly detected by the cat's organ of Jacobson, are sufficient to keep it on the correct course. Just a few molecules of a familiar smell could be sufficient to guide the cat home with the pinpoint accuracy of a landing beacon bringing a jet aircraft down on the runway.

Another skill which may well assist the cat is its ability to note the passing of time with considerable accuracy. This would allow it to calculate how much ground had been covered, and so work out how far was left to travel.

But a sense of smell and time can only be of use once the cat is heading along the right route, since any error at the start of its journey would make it impossible ever to return home.

If we want to travel across unfamiliar country, our ability to think and reason allows us to choose between a wide range of options. We could read a map, use a compass or sextant, navigate by the stars or simply ask for directions. But suppose that, like Herrick's cats, we are stranded in strange surroundings miles from home with only our natural sense of direction to guide us. Imagine, for instance, that you are a kidnap victim who has been blindfolded, driven over a zig-zag route for miles and then released into a featureless landscape. How accurately could you head off in the direction that would eventually lead to your own front door?

You may be surprised to learn that you'd probably do reasonably well and stand a good chance of working out the correct route home. And in this inborn human ability to navigate accurately without artificial aids may be found at least part of the explanation for a cat's homing skills. For a basic assumption behind this research is that whatever innate powers we possess are almost certain to be present to an even greater extent in animals.

One scientist who has long suspected that man and animals use the same sort of mechanisms to find their way around is Dr. Robin Baker, a lecturer in zoology at the University of Manchester in England. He first began to put his theories to the test in 1976 when he took a number of third-year zoology students from the university on a mystery tour with a difference. Not only did none of his volunteers know where they were going, but they weren't told where they were when they arrived.

The students were first blindfolded and then driven by van over a complex and tortuous route for distances of between four and forty miles from the campus. On arrival they were taken from the van and, before having the blindfolds removed, asked first to say in which direction they thought the university lay from their position and then to point in that direction. After this, they were allowed to take off their blindfolds and asked, once again, to point toward the university.

Dr. Baker's first surprise came when he found, contrary to expectations, that direction-finding was extremely accurate while the blindfolds remained in place but declined sharply as soon as they had been removed. Somehow the students had been able to follow all the turns and twists of the outward trip, despite not being allowed to see the passing countryside. Yet restoring their sight left them confused and uncertain about where they were.

When asked how they knew in which direction to point, none of the subjects could provide a satisfactory answer. Some claimed they knew which way they were traveling from the sun's heat on their faces, others explained that because they knew all the roads in the area so well it hadn't been too hard for them to reconstruct the route in their imagination. The majority admitted, however, that they quickly became lost and were unable to work out where they were.

When the van stopped and they were asked to state which direction the university lay in, they simply guessed and were as amazed as the researchers that their spontaneous response proved so uncannily correct.

Dr. Baker was soon able to eliminate the sun as a factor, since his subjects' accuracy was just as high on overcast as on fine days. Those who claimed to be familiar with the countryside did neither better nor worse in the direction-finding tasks than those who confessed to be completely lost. Even more intriguing was the fact that accuracy did not decrease as the distance from the campus increased. In fact just the reverse happened: after about three miles the direction was pinpointed with even greater success on trips of up to forty miles.

In a more sophisticated version of the early experiments, Dr. Baker used thirty boys and girls aged sixteen to seventeen. This time, in addition to blindfolds, his subjects wore astronaut-style helmets, half containing genuine bar magnets and the remainder fakes. The helmet wearers did not know, of course, whether the magnets were real or dummies.

Dr. Baker's plan was to see whether a powerful magnetic source would somehow jam the brain's built-in homing system. The results confirmed his theory that magnetism did indeed interfere with natural navigational ability. Subjects who wore genuine magnets on their helmets consistently made an error of nearly 90 degrees counterclockwise on the direction-finding tests.

Later the experiments were repeated using more sophisticated battery-powered magnets in an electronic circuit, which reduced the magnetic field at the center of the helmet to about three times that of the Earth. And an added refinement was the ability to reverse the direction of current through the coils, or deactivate them completely without the subjects being aware of what was happening.

Using this equipment, Dr. Baker carried out a series of experiments in the autumn of 1979 which conclusively demonstrated that humans really do possess a magnetic sense of direction. He has also discovered that the sense is not active when we are asleep and that women seem to rely more on their mental magnetism when finding their way around unfamiliar territory than do men. "As we move around within our environment, we make unknowing use of magnetic sense," comments Dr. Baker.

Today more than half a dozen laboratories around the world are actively studying the phenomenon and attempting to identify the area of the brain involved.

Animals and birds are also known to use some form of

built-in compass for navigation. Two German scientists, Drs. Roswitha and Wolfgang Wiltschlka, have shown, for instance, that when homing pigeons are subjected to a changing magnetic field on their way to the release site, they often become disoriented and fly away in the wrong direction.

Navigation by means of the earth's magnetic pole, as we do when using a compass, may not be the only way animals use magnetism for finding their way around, however. It also seems likely that they can follow so-called ley-lines, invisible paths which many people believe link such landmarks as old churches, ancient mounds, prehistoric sites and standing stones.

The idea that these familiar features of the British landscape might really be signposts marking out very old, straight tracks crisscrossing the countryside first occurred to a sixty-five-year-old Hereford brewer named Alfred Watkins as he was riding his horse across the Welch hills. Watkins's sudden revelation was that, just as the landscape was crossed by visible pathways, lanes and highways it might also be marked out by invisible tracks which he called "leys." Before long, "ley-hunting," although considered by many scientists to be a pursuit for cranks, attracted widespread popular interest. This was heightened still further during the 1960s when an official dowser with the British Museum, Captain Robert Boothby, published a theory which claimed that prehistoric sites were crossed by underground streams which could be detected using a dowsing rod.

One man who was sufficiently intrigued to do his own exploration of such sites, using the traditional hazel dowsing rod, was a lawyer named Guy Underwood. He confirmed Robert Boothby's findings but also discovered that there were additional underground streams associated with ancient sites. Along these flowed not water but magnetic energy. The water lines exerted a negative force on the dowsing rod (the pull was mainly on the left hand), while the magnetic tracks, of which there were several running in parallel like railway lines, exerted a positive force by pulling the rod to the right.

Underwood also noticed that wild animals followed these invisible tracks as they moved around their territories. Convinced that he had stumbled upon a principle of nature which science had so far failed to recognize, he wrote: "The main characteristics are that it appears to be generated within the Earth, and to cause wave motion perpendicular to the Earth's surface; that it has great penetrative power; that it affects the nerve cells of animals . . ."

There is a link here with the well-established phenomenon of dowsing for water, which depends on the sensitivity of the human nervous system to changes and distortions in the surrounding electrical field caused by variations in the ground conditions. When the dowser's twig twists in response to a subterranean stream, for example, his muscles are contracting due to the influence of local change in the pattern of electrical forces.

All this may seem to have taken us a long way from cats and their incredible journeys, but in fact invisible magnetic paths, familiar perhaps to our ancient ancestors who marked them by monuments and standing stones, but lost to modern knowledge, could prove an important piece in the complex jigsaw puzzle of skills which make up the cat's homing instinct. Perhaps cats are able to detect and follow these ley-lines in exactly the same way that a motorist relies on the thin lines of colored ink which represent roads on his road map.

When first starting a journey homeward, it may be that the cat gets a general direction from its built-in compass.

This tells it, for example, that it must head northeast, or southwest. Once the journey has begun, however, the cat picks up the powerful magnetic signal from a subterranean ley-line which is heading in the right general direction and keeps on course by reference to this unseen track. The closer it gets to home, the easier such navigation becomes, because the landscape grows increasingly familiar. Trees, bushes, streets and buildings are beginning to match the mental map formed of visual memories and these recollections of the route are powerfully reinforced by the different odors associated with home.

This combination of skills seems to provide at least part of the answer to the mystery of Type I homing. But Type II journeys are far harder to explain. Here, remember, the cat begins in familiar surroundings and sets off into unknown terrain. The question now is not only how he knows where he is, but even more importantly, how does he know where to go?

What unique powers directed Beau Chat to the very school where his mistress worked and her son studied?

How did Pitchou, Cindy and Sugar know what trail to follow in the search for their owners? The French vet's suggestion that the kitten followed his master's scent along the railway lines is, of course, not in the least credible. There would be no such trail to follow.

Since these stories are, frequently, so well-authenticated and supported by such strong evidence that they cannot be explained away by deception or delusion, we may have to seek solutions in the realm of the paranormal to try to discover some psychic bond between animal and owner which allows the cat to identify the correct address out of, perhaps, millions of other addresses in a strange city.

One scientist who has no hesitation in turning to ESP to provide the answer is Dr. Joseph Rhine. He believes that not only do cats possess some psychic powers but that these offer the only possible explanation for Type II homing. Dr. Rhine points out that the question of *psi* in animals originated among zoologists who were attempting to solve the mystery of these incredible journeys. Such eminent biologists as Professors A.C. Hardy and Julian Huxley also accepted that psychic powers must be taken into account as a standard source of explanation in animal research.

"Zoologists have shown no lack of readiness to discuss the ESP hypothesis in connection with the unexplained behavior of animals in finding their way in unfamiliar territory," comments Dr. Rhine. Indeed, this pioneer of extrasensory studies sees in the homing skills of animals a unique opportunity for investigating paranormal powers.

"*Psi* would seem to be involved with much greater magnitude and consistency than it is even in the spontaneous experiences of humans," he comments. "The reliability of *psi* capacity to guide an animal such as Sugar in making the countless daily decisions necessary in a 1,500-mile trip would be of an order so great as to suggest even that some qualitative differences in ability might be involved."

Testing any possible psychic involvement is, of course, extremely difficult and to date nobody has been able to come up with convincing evidence that telepathy, clairvoyance, precognition or any of the other paranormal skills we considered in the previous chapter is involved.

While many facts about Type II homing point strongly in this direction, a full understanding will have to wait until such time as we achieve greater insight into the nature of forces which appear to defy the laws of nature.

For cats to rejoin their owners over vast distances takes more than just a good sense of direction, of course. To sustain this desire for a reunion over the months or even years which a long trek takes points to powerful motivation, great determination and considerable resourcefulness.

In order to survive on the long journeys, the cats must find, along the way, many people prepared to feed them and probably to offer them a comfortable home. Yet, while accepting what is necessary to sustain them in their quest, these animals turned their backs time and time again on a life of security and ease to head forever onward into the unknown.

So what makes a particular person or specific family so important that this potent urge for reunion arises?

CHAPTER 8

What Cats Tell Us About Ourselves

The mysterious world of dreams, our ancient ancestors' unrecorded history, searches for lost civilizations and the puzzle of how children learn mathematics—four fascinating and important research areas with one common link. The vital role being played by the cat in expanding human knowledge.

For many years now, cats have been the focus of interest for researchers in such diverse fields as psychology, anthropology, archaeology, biology and the neurosciences. For despite the fact that these creatures possess powers which are, in many ways, far superior to our own, they may also hold the key which could unlock many secrets of mankind's past, present and future.

Let's start by looking at the way in which cats are being used to help scientists unravel the mystery of sleeping and dreaming, an experience shared by us all, yet still far from being properly understood.

Dreaming

The Sleepwalking Cats

While watching a sleeping cat, you may have noticed his tail start flicking or seen his paws twitch excitedly and wondered whether those movements might not mean he was dreaming. Were his whiskers quivering with anticipation as he stalked prey through a tangle of undergrowth? Was he running to greet a friend in his imagination?

For thousands of years people have observed animals in sleep and wondered whether they shared our experience of dreams. Nearly 2,000 years ago, indeed, Petronius Arbiter, a nobleman in the court of the Emperor Nero, reflected this popular interest among philosophers when he wrote: "... *et canis in somnis leporis vestigia lustrat*" ("and the dog in sleep crosses the hare's tracks").

While it is tempting to assume that any physical movements must be the outward and visible reflection of inward and invisible dreaming, this is misleading where cats are concerned. For the most significant feature of their dreams is not movement at all but a state of deep (hyper) relaxation known technically as postural atonia. While dreams dance through his brain, the cat rolls over on one side and, although the paws may occasionally flex and the tail, ears or whiskers quiver, the most significant indication of dreaming is this utterly slack and relaxed condition.

Dreams in Cats and Men

Scientists offer two explanations for the mechanisms of dreaming. The first proposes that, like a spectator in some cerebral cinema, we watch a chain of images unfold on a kind of mental movie screen. Support for this idea comes from the fact that while dreaming, the eyelids of both hu-

mans and cats move rapidly beneath closed lids as though
swiftly scanning some internal images.

An alternative theory suggests that, rather than being the
result of stimulation of the visual cortex (that part of the
brain which enables us to see while awake), dreams are
programmed by an as-yet-undiscovered part of the brain
whose identification would prove a major advance in solving the mystery not only of why we dream but why we
need to sleep at all.

Is sleeping necessary to repair the wear and tear of
everyday activities, the "chief nourisher in life's feast,"
as Macbeth described it? Are dreams the brain's method
for eliminating unwanted memories and undesirable
thoughts, as Dr. Francis Crick and Dr. Graeme Mitchison
from the Cambridge Molecular Biology Laboratory have
argued? It is in search of answers to these intriguing questions that researchers have turned to the cat for assistance.

The Patterns of Dreams

Research into sleep and dreams is usually conducted in a
sleep laboratory, typically two rooms separated by a wall
with a two-way observation mirror in the dividing wall.
One is equipped with cameras, chart recorders and a piece
of brain-monitoring equipment known as an electroenceph-
alogram (EEG). This detects the electrical activity inside
the brain and prints it out in the form of wave patterns on
continuously moving chart paper.

Apart from the mirror and a tangled skein of fine wires
leading to a large junction box on the wall, it might be a
perfectly ordinary, if somewhat austere, bedroom. It is
here, every night, that volunteers fall asleep in the cause
of science with small electrodes attached to their heads.
These carry information, via the confusion of cables, to the

EEG equipment next door the moment the subject drifts off to sleep.

When a subject first gets into bed, the pen recorders flick urgently backward and forward, creating a permanent record of the alert and active brain. As he gets drowsy, entering what researchers call Stage 1 sleep, the wave patterns start to change. In Stage 2, deeper sleep, the trace consists of a characteristic wave pattern called "spindles," while Stages 3 and 4 are usually grouped together as Slow Wave Sleep, also known as orthodox sleep. These stages are revealed by a trace containing large, sweeping, low-frequency waves. Beyond Stage 4 lies the land of dreams, as the brain shifts into an even lower gear.

Now, although the subject is deeply asleep and very hard to arouse, the electrical activity produced shows a wave form similar to that found in wakeful people. For this reason the dreaming stage is sometimes known as paradoxical sleep. In this state, heartbeat and breathing are irregular, the body relaxed with muscles flaccid. The most important physical response, however, is the rapid to-and-fro movement of the eyes. This burst of activity, which occurs between 5 and 30 times per minute, has led researchers to refer to the dreaming state as the REM (Rapid Eye Movement) stage of sleep. If a person is shaken back into consciousness during REM sleep, he will invariably report having been dreaming. In humans, orthodox and paradoxical (REM) sleep alternate in cycles lasting around 90 minutes and producing three or four periods of dreaming during the average night's rest.

The link between REM sleep and dreaming was first identified during the mid-1950s by two Chicago researchers, Dr. Nathaniel Kleitman and Dr. Aserinsky, while they were studying the sleep patterns of very young children. They observed hourly periods of restlessness in infants during which they also noted that the eyes moved urgently beneath closed lids. A third member of their team, Dr. Bill Dement, then developed a method of recording the changes in electrical potential caused by such movements with the use of delicate silver electrodes.

With these detectors in place, the researchers were able to investigate the mental state of sleepers during the REM stage by the simple process of waking them up and asking if they had been dreaming. More than 80 percent of those awoken at this point confirmed that they had been in the middle of a dream.

Why Cats Have Proved So Helpful

Cats are the world's greatest sleepers. They spend around two-thirds of their lives asleep, double the time of any other mammal. Why they should need so much sleep remains a puzzle, although the amount required is known to be influenced by such factors as the cat's age, sexual arousal, the weather and hunger—the greatest promoters of sleep being a warm bed in secure surroundings following a good meal. Typically, they take short catnaps throughout the day, although when an owner spends most of the day away from the home, the cat may snooze continuously in his absence, being alert and active only during the morning and evening.

When Dr. Dement investigated sleeping cats, he discovered a pattern of electrical activity in the brain similar to that found in human sleeping. By painlessly fastening lightweight electrodes to an animal's head, he showed that the EEG of a waking cat has no particular pattern, since it changes continuously with the creature's state of arousal and events in its surroundings. If something happens to catch the cat's attention, for example, the sudden alertness will be faithfully recorded on the charts. As the cat becomes drowsy and falls asleep, the brain waves generated are slow and irregular. The muscles of neck and trunk often remain tense at this stage and the cat is instantly awakened by the click of the latch or the squeak of a mouse.

Between fifteen and thirty minutes after falling asleep, the cat relaxes and the eyes start their rapid movements. At the same time the body relaxes very deeply, while the EEG shows the pattern of wakeful brain waves associated with paradoxical sleep. Six to seven minutes after this, the cat returns to shallow sleep and spends another thirty minutes in this state before dreaming again. Research has shown that a fit, mature cat will spend around 15 percent of its life in deep sleep and 50 percent in shallow sleep. Kittens, on the other hand, never experience shallow sleep during the first month of life.

Is the cat dreaming? And if so, can we ever know the content of those dreams? Answers to these intriguing questions have now been produced by the brilliant studies of Professor Michel Jouvet at Claude-Bernard University in Lyons, France. He was interested in the cat's hyper-relaxed condition, the "postural atonia" which characterizes dream states. This, Jouvet concluded, was a way of safeguarding the animal against possible injuries caused if it were to physically act out its dreams. Jouvet also discovered that the cat's REM stage was related to a particular sort of brain activity known as PGO waves.*

This led him to wonder what would happen if a cat's brain had been damaged so that the mechanism which produces the hyper-relaxed condition no longer functions.

*PGO stands for pons, lateral geniculate and occipital regions of the cortex. The waves are the result of irregular firings of the nerve cells in those three areas of the brain. They are known to be connected with sleep but their purpose is not fully understood by scientists.

When cats with such injuries were studied, they showed no differences in waking behavior, playing, eating, mating and socializing exactly like normal animals. As soon as REM sleep starts, however, differences between the intact and brain-injured cats become immediately obvious. Instead of relaxing deeply, these animals turned into sleepwalkers and started acting out their dreams.

Sometimes, although still deeply asleep, the cat would rise to its feet and crouch low, stalking a prey which existed only in its dreams. On other occasions it might start turning its head to and fro, as though following the movements of a passing human. Occasionally the cats went off in search of food or began playing with an invisible toy, pausing now and then to lick and groom themselves.

That the cats were still fast asleep was confirmed by the fact that the pupils were still covered by the third eyelid† (normally a sign of deep slumber) and by the results of simple tests, such as pulling an object across in front of them to see if they followed it with their gaze. Finally, when Jouvet injected a drug, such as the antibiotic chloramphenicol, which prevents REM sleep, the movements ceased entirely.

One explanation for this behavior is that the cat's visual system is being stimulated and this produces hallucinations which the animal then acts out. This view corresponds to a belief that human dreaming involves viewing a sort of mental movie.

Professor Jouvet, however, feels that this appealingly common-sense notion is incorrect. He found that Rapid Eye Movements typically begin some twenty minutes before the start of brain activity linked to dreaming, so cannot

†The third eyelid, which is also called the nictitating membrane, or haw, consists of a third fold of skin that moves swiftly and diagonally across the eye underneath the eyelid and helps to lubricate the cornea.

be a response to visual hallucinations. A more probable theory, in his view, is that those parts of the brain which generate the PGO waves are also responsible for programming dreams in cats and, perhaps, in humans.

Because brain-injured cats act out their dreams in this way, scientists have been able to note exactly when dreaming occurs while simultaneously recording brain waves. This allows them to determine the association in time between the two measures not obtainable by simply waking up humans and asking them to recall their dreams.

Thanks to the cat, therefore, sleep researchers have been able to take us a small but important step forward in achieving a clearer understanding of the process of dreaming. At the same time their research has provided answers to questions that have tantalized cat-owners down the centuries. We now know that cats do, indeed, dream and that those dreams relate to activities in their daily lives.

Cats on the Trail of History

While psychologists and neurologists have been monitoring the electrical activity of cat brains in order to explore the realm of dreams, anthropologists and geneticists have been using these animals as living history books on which is written the saga of human migration, exploration and exploitation during periods for which no other reliable record exists.

A study of the distribution of cats allows specialists to gain knowledge on such matters as the growth and development of commerce, the triumphant advance of conquerors and the terrified flights of the vanquished, the rise of civilizations and the collapse of cultures.

All these, and much else of great historical significance,

may be discovered by the quick, simple and economical process of examining the cats' coats, markings and colors, and by looking for any general physical abnormalities or congenital handicaps. All these features are written into the cat's genes, the blueprint which determines the outward appearance of the animal, and in this way the creature's genetic heritage becomes a living testament to mankind's distant past.

To understand why this should be the case, we need only consider some of the basic facts about the long association between ourselves and cats. This relationship, which, as we saw, goes back at least 4,000 years, has survived the rise and fall of empires, the disappearance of once-mighty states and the gradual expansion of man's influence over the whole surface of the globe.

Almost from the first, cats shared human habitation to a considerable extent. The ancient cities of Alexandria and Carthage, for example, had cat populations of more than 100,000. Since cats had become increasingly dependent on humans, they seldom wandered far from home, and because they had little commercial value there were no financial or social incentives to encourage selective breeding.

While dogs have been selectively bred for thousands of years, it was not until the end of the nineteenth century that the same attention was paid to cats, and it is only within the past decade or so that any efforts have been made to create cats with particular types of personality and temperament. Because of this, mutant genes, which produce variations, occur less often among cats than dogs, leading to a smaller number of breeds. Furthermore, although the cat possesses a vast quantity of genes, relatively few are concerned with the physical features that collectively define a breed. Most are concerned with ensuring that the cat's bodily functions remain superbly effective.

Cats have other advantages as well, related to the fact that they show variable traits (polymorphism) whose genetic basis is fairly well understood. Seven out of ten of these traits are concerned with the pattern, texture and color of the coat and so may be identified and classified with ease.

Cats have been spread by man from their original homelands to every part of the world and can even be found in areas now abandoned by human habitation. This has meant that their distinctive markings, of which they have several, result from mutations which occurred during the period when those particular cats lived among a specific group of people within a fairly limited geographical area. As those people migrated, to open commercial routes, expand into fresh territories through trade or conquest, establish new settlements or flee from the crumbling remains of decaying civilizations, many took their cats with them. In this way the dispersion of a particular type of marking tells us where people from different parts of the world migrated to.

How Cat Coats Reveal Our Past

If you notice that a particular coat color or pattern is found throughout a certain area, or different areas, you can be fairly confident that an associated group of people lived, or moved through, the area at some time, leaving behind traces of their own culture, features of their language, art and architecture, their beliefs, superstitions, legends and skills.

One of the leading workers in the field of cat genetics, Dr. Neil Todd, director of the Carnivore Genetics Research Center of Illinois, notes that the ginger cat is distributed in Europe along a fairly narrow, irregular corridor linking London to the Mediterranean. This has, for centuries, been a popular and highly developed commercial route followed by traders as an alternative to transporting goods through the Straits of Gibraltar. The fact that fewer such cats are to be found in Rome and Marseilles, however, indicates that this line of foreign immigration exerted much less influence in that part of Europe where the native Romans remained dominant.

Finally, a high concentration of these cats along the northern coast of Africa indicates that the population route, and hence the culture and commercial influences, extended to that continent as well.

Dr. Todd also suggests that the large numbers of nearly-white cats found in Scotland, Iceland, the Faroe Islands and the Isle of Man are associated with the Viking migrations some thousand years ago. These cats are also to be found in the Van area of Turkey, which is also the home of the celebrated Turkish Swimming Cat, revealing that the Vikings almost certainly visited this area of the world and perhaps even settled there.

In New England, New Brunswick and Nova Scotia, animals with an extra toe make up more than 1 in 10 of the cat population. Apart from a few isolated pockets, however, these cats are rare away from those areas, showing that the focus for the spread of extra-toed cats was New England, where they were probably first bred as a novelty. The cats must have been present in Boston by the mid-eighteenth century, since they are equally abundant in present-day Halifax, a city not founded until the middle of the eighteenth century, when it became a refuge for thousands of Loyalists fleeing from the American War of Independence, who presumably took their unusual cats with them.

The History of Cats

The first record of cats being domesticated for the benefit of man comes, as we saw, from Egypt around 3000 B.C. where they protected granaries from rats and mice. But it is just possible that they shared man's home far earlier than this. Feline bones discovered in the dwellings of ancient cavemen have been presumed to be those of wild cats. Now, thanks to a remarkable scientific breakthrough, it would be possible to discover whether that assumption is correct.

Egyptian cats were derived from the African wildcat, a gray animal with blackish stripes and spots on the body and legs, dusky feet and a black-tipped tail with several rings. The hair was short and the general build resembled that of the common house cat.

From Egypt cats came to Italy, in the company of Phoenician traders, and became settled inhabitants long before the birth of Christ. Soon they were spreading throughout Europe and breeding with the European wildcat, a closely related species which has longer fur and tail. The Egyptian wildcat has completely black pads to the feet, with this coloring extending as far as the heel. In the European cat this black is restricted to a small, round spot on the pads. Domestic cats with wild coloring have markings on the hind feet which correspond to the original Egyptian pattern.

The cat's origins can also be traced from the markings of the so-called tabby, the basic "wild type" from which all the others have evolved. This is, indeed, the universal cat, since every other breed, even the most elegant and aristocratic, remains a tabby at heart. However, it is the tiger-striped (mackerel) rather than the more widely known blotched (classic) pattern that is the true descendant of the original wild cat. The striped type is found in both European and African wildcats, while the less distinct type results from a mutation. Underlying each is a gray camouflaging pattern found in many mammals, especially the rabbit. The hairs actually have a bluish base and black tips separated by yellow bands, but because these slope backwards, the overall effect is a freckled grayish coloring which helps the animal to blend with the background. The stripes are also used for purposes of camouflage in much the same way that army combat uniforms break up the overall olive green or gray with blotches, stripes or other confusing patterns. These markings were passed down to the domestic tabby from its wild ancestors, as was length of hair—shorthaired species from the European wildcat, *Felis silvestris*, and the long-haired variety from Persia and Afghanistan.

The British Shorthair, the most popular pet in England and the U.S., is descended from animals who accompanied the Roman legions on their conquest of the islands. Once established, the cat proved such a valuable creature that, in A.D. 936, Howell the Good, prince of south central Wales, passed a law for the protection of both cats and kittens.

Long-haired cats, often referred to as Persians, have been popular in Britain for around eighty years, with the long-haired black cat being one of the oldest of the pedigree breeds.

Another long-haired breed, the blue-eyed white, probably originated in the Middle East, where records of their presence going back more than three centuries have been found. From Persia they came to France and were, at first, called Angoras, the term Persian only being introduced later. Another genetic similarity in these cats is that many of the breed are partially or, in most cases, completely deaf. This is caused by a degeneration of the inner ear resulting from a defect associated with the dominant white gene and especially affects blue-eyed whites, although both orange and odd-eyed cats may be similarly disabled.

It is important to appreciate that following the movements of a people by studying genetic variations in local cat populations depends on the outward characteristics of these animals rather than their breed names. The Abyssinian, for example, is not a native of that country, which probably never has had its own species of cat. The first Abyssinian seen in England is believed to have been a cat named Zula, imported into England soon after the end of the Abyssinian War by a certain Mrs. Lennard, the wife of a serving officer.

The tailless Manx cat is common in the Far East, predominating in Malay and the Philippines where long-tailed animals are seldom seen. In New England and the mid-Atlantic states of America, the Manx is sometimes called a "rabbit cat," because some people believed, on the basis of its lack of tail and a coat which is longer and looser than in other cats, that it must be part-cat and part-rabbit. It is not yet known whether the Manx reached the Isle of Man from outside, or arose on the island as the result of some spontaneous mutation.

Probably the most intriguing domestic breed is the Siamese, characterized by the frequent appearance of kinked tails and cross-eyes, defects which breeders find hard to eliminate from the strain. This appears to be caused by abnormal nerve connections between eyes and brain, caused by a harmful gene which results in double vision. The cat squints in an attempt to correct this defect.

The most popular breed of pedigree cat, held by many to represent the epitome of grace and elegance, the Siamese came to the West from Siam (now Thailand) in 1884, although it was not native to the country and, indeed, is only rarely seen there today.

The Thais sometimes call it the Chinese cat, although the evidence suggests that the mutation first arose from Siam, or close by, rather than across the border. When the mutation first arose is not known, although the character- istic pattern was recognized as a distinct type in Siam cen- turies before the breed arrived in England. Ancient records show that they were kept as pets by residents of Siam's ancient capital, Ayudha, founded in 1350 and razed to the ground by invading Burmese troops some four hundred years later.

It was often called the Royal Cat of Siam, from the fact that noble families were willing to spend the large sums needed for any which became available.

The *Cat-Book Poems*, one of the documents salvaged from the smoldering ruins of Ayudha, describes seal-point Siamese as possessing black tails, feet and ears with white hair and reddish eyes.

The first Siamese to set foot on British soil, who arrived in 1884, are often claimed to be Pho and Mia, a pair ob- tained by Owen Gould, the British consul-general in Bang- kok, as a present for his sister. These were later exhibited at the 1885 Crystal Palace cat show, where they are said to have attracted considerable interest. The records show, however, that Siamese cats had been exhibited, fourteen years earlier, at the first cat show run on modern lines held in 1871. Then, however, they found little popularity, being described by one writer as an "unnatural, nightmare kind of cat."

Following the 1885 show, however, more pairs were imported and reached America in 1890, a gift, it is said, from the King of Siam to a friend.

By the late nineteenth century almost a dozen Siamese

were being shown, in two special classes, at the annual Crystal Palace cat show. The early cats, imported directly from Siam, were different in appearance from those bred in Britain. Their heads were rounder, their coats darker and their tails were often so deformed as to resemble a corkscrew. The first arrivals had delicate health, produced small litters of kittens and died early as a result of the cold, damp climate. Gradually, however, the breed grew hardier, developing a thick protective winter coat. Even today, though, Siamese adore the heat, happily lying against a radiator which is almost too hot to be touched by a human hand.

The history of the cat, written into their genes and expressed in distinctive markings is, therefore, in a very real sense the history of the human race. As the science of feline genetics develops more sophisticated techniques for monitoring their distribution, we can expect to learn even more about our past.

The Secrets of the Bones

So far we have only looked at the information to be derived from the study of living cats, but even fragments of their skeletons can prove highly revealing, as work by three researchers, Dr. Isabella Drew, director of the Sackler Laboratory of the Department of Art History and Archaeology at Columbia University, and her colleagues Dr. Dexter Perkins and Patricia Daly have shown.

A few years ago they developed a technique for telling whether ancient bones belonged to a wild or a domesticated animal. After examining hundreds of specimens of both kinds, all many thousands of years old, they were able to pinpoint a crucial structural difference relating to the distribution of crystals used to give the bones additional strength.

In pets, these are located around the joints, while in wild animals they are far more diffusely distributed. Special microscopic viewing techniques make these differences immediately and dramatically apparent. When small sections of bones from a domestic animal are placed on the microscope stage and then illuminated in a certain way, they show up as a brilliant red which turns blue and yellow if the slide is rotated through 90 degrees. These colors are not found when wild animal bones are examined in the same way.

One theory put forward to explain these differences is that the diet of wild animals allows them to construct bones strong enough to function without the additional structural reinforcement which the crystal lattice provides. Domestic animals, because their diets are, in some ways, less satisfactory, have to develop bones with additional reinforcement around the joints.

Although this discovery may not, at first sight, seem especially exciting, its implications for archaeology and anthropology are considerable. For the keeping of pets, especially cats, reflects a certain level of civilization, suggesting settled life-styles and a particular attitude toward animals.

If those cat bones discovered in the ancient cave dwellings turned out to have come from domesticated rather than wild animals, for instance, it would cast a fascinating new light on the private lives of our early ancestors. From primitive savages, they are transformed into more domesticated and settled beings capable of enjoying an affectionate relationship with animals rather than regarding them solely as a source of fur or food.

Even more dramatically, the identification of bone fragments as coming from tame (rather than wild) cats might one day allow archaeologists to discover lost civilizations that would otherwise remain buried beneath shifting desert sands or concealed behind the lush growth of jungles.

If cat bones were found in an area which showed no other traces of human settlement, and these turned out to be from a domesticated animal, it would be reasonable to assume that people once lived close to that spot. A more detailed search could then be made of the immediate vicinity with the strong possibility that other remains would be unearthed.

When dating techniques for these bones have been developed, the remains should also tell us exactly when that settlement flourished. If sufficient parts of the skeleton can be discovered, it may also prove possible to identify the mutant strain, through differences in skull shape, average size of bones, tooth formation and so on, which would enable researchers to reconstruct the migration routes taken by those who once lived there.

Counting with Cats

Here's a simple problem: multiply 3 by 4, add 2 and subtract 1. The answer is, of course, 13, and I am sure you had no difficulty in working it out. But now I'd like you to reflect on just how you solved that sum. It's almost certain you used *words* when thinking about those figures; that, in your head, you said something like: "Three times four is twelve, plus two gives fourteen and take away one to leave thirteen."

This is the way most people do arithmetic, and the way most children are taught to think about numbers, which makes life difficult for psychologists and educators interested in figuring out how the human mind tackles number problems. Even if you try to get people to provide the answers to such problems without speaking, by using counters or fingers for instance, you can never be certain that words are not getting in on the act somehow.

So is our counting ability firmly, and inevitably, rooted in language?

If we knew the answer to this question it could have important practical benefits, for instance in teaching children arithmetic. Should schools adopt a strongly language-based approach in which, for example, children learn their number tables by chanting "two times two is four," and so on in the traditional way? Or is manipulating numbers an intellectual task so different from working with words that thinking about them with language makes our mathematical reasoning less efficient than it could be?

Perhaps children should be taught to do their sums using a completely different, nonverbal, approach.

In their search for an answer to this problem, psychologists have tried studying infants before they develop language. The difficulty here, of course, is to obtain a response of any kind from a baby given a simple counting task. One way is to condition an eye-blink response in the infant by blowing a puff of air into the eyes. If this is preceded by some stimulus, such as presenting the child with two dots on a card, it eventually learns to blink, in the absence of any puff of air, whenever the dots are presented. Now the child is shown a card with three dots. The crucial test is whether or not it can distinguish between the two stimulus cards. In other words, does it "know" the difference between two and three? If it does, there will be no eye-blink to the three-dot card and the child can be said to have some innate, non-language-dependent, counting skill.

But although a reasonable approach in theory, in practice it is often extremely hard to condition the eye-blink, or any other response, and the whole experiment is fraught with difficulties.

Now cats are helping to provide some answers through the studies of Dr. Jules Masserman, M.D., and Dr. David Rubinfine of the Department of Psychiatry at the University of Chicago.* They have developed a simple counting experiment in which they trained a small group of cats to lift the lid of a box in order to get a morsel of their favorite food. The cats were taught to do this each time a light flashed or a bell sounded. Once they were responding almost perfectly, they were taught to open the boxes by pressing a small wooden pedal. Next they had to learn to press the pedal twice in order to get the lid off. The number of pedal pushes needed was gradually increased, obliging the cat to count if it wanted a tasty snack. Some animals proved extremely skilled at this task, one of them, described as a "mixed-breed alley variety, male" showing a substantial superiority over the others.

When the number of presses was increased to three, the cats were initially puzzled and frustrated by their failure to raise the lid after two presses, but it did not take long for most to work out what was required.

The results of this experiment reveal that counting can indeed take place in the absence of language. One long-time advocate of the "nonverbal" approach to learning numbers is the American psychologist Glenn Doman, whose methods have been used by many thousands of parents on both sides of the Atlantic to teach infants only a few months old to recognize, and manipulate, numbers presented as dots on cards.

---

*Like all lower animals, cats are not thought capable of using symbolic language, in the way that humans and possibly some primates do, since they lack the specialized language centers, usually found on the left side of the human brain, which are considered essential for verbal reasoning.

The results of this work, together with the outcome of laboratory experiments using cats, might eventually lead to a revolution in the classroom and make the rote learning of multiplication tables seem as old-fashioned as chalk and slates.

CHAPTER 9

The Social Life of Your Pet

Not long ago, a friend told me a feline horror story which will, I am sure, sound familiar to a great many cat-owners. After being scolded for some minor misdemeanor, her pet disappeared from home. About thirty minutes later, she returned looking very pleased with herself and began meowing for attention. Then she proudly led her owner into the garden where a peace offering was on display. Neatly laid out beneath an apple tree were the corpses of five young pigeons, fledglings which, my friend immediately realized, could only have come from the loft of her next-door neighbor.

Her immediate feelings of revulsion and anger at such an apparently wanton act of slaughter may seem perfectly reasonable to other humans, but such a reaction can only have left her cat with a sense of bewildered hurt. For while most cat-owners, not unreasonably, feel distressed when confronted by the grisly remains of their cat's latest hunting

165

expedition, they ought to be flattered by such a mark of the creature's high esteem. By presenting them with a mangled starling or headless mouse, the cat is offering a gesture of affection and gratitude. For in the world of cats, a gift of food has a very special meaning. It's their way of saying thank you for the care they have been given and an acknowledgment of their obligation to keep the larder filled with freshly killed meat in return for meals already received.

By these actions cats allow owners an intimate glimpse into their strange, secret and highly structured private world.

The Society of Cats

Cats are often considered remote, aloof creatures and they certainly are much more independent in their outlook than most domesticated animals. But it would be a serious mistake to regard them as unfriendly loners. Apart from hunting forays, which are generally solitary affairs, cats are gregarious creatures whose social organization in the wild is among the most complicated and intelligent of any in the animal kingdom.

Within the cat pack, which may number a hundred or more animals, there exist many clearly defined roles, a great deal of mutual cooperation, considerable affection between individual members and an ethical concept of shared obligations. The contrast between their society and that of dogs is considerable, since, in their wild state, dogs form smaller groups, show less cooperation, and communicate ideas, intentions and desires less effectively.

Much of our knowledge about the private life of cats,

wild, feral* and domesticated, comes from the studies of ethologists, specialists in animal behavior, who prefer to make observations under natural conditions rather than perform stringently controlled experiments in a laboratory. They have tracked cats with cameras and binoculars, watched their activities after dark using infrared lamps or light-intensification lenses capable of transforming night into day, and even fastened lightweight radio transmitter collars around their necks in order to trail them over long distances without interference.

Thanks to their efforts, a great deal is now known about cat society and much of what we have learned can help owners gain a clearer understanding of their pets' desires and needs.

Why Cats Banded Together

Cats first formed colonies thousands of years before they were encouraged to share human habitation. In the wilderness, cooperation and the creation of well-structured groups was more than a matter of convenience, it was the secret of survival.

Compared with other predators, cats start out with several serious disadvantages. Being small, light and not very strong, the range of food available to them is limited. Contrary to popular belief, they are not even ruthlessly efficient killers. More than 90 percent of the birds they stalk are able to escape, while a mouse has a 1 in 5 chance of surviving the encounter.

By way of compensation, evolution led to the development of brain rather than brawn, great agility, extremely powerful senses and an instinctive desire to form support-

*Feral cats are once-domesticated animals who have reverted to the wild.

ive groups. Mutual aid for the common good is a skill at which cats excel.

This emphasis on cooperation may appear to overlook the caterwauling cries of cats fighting by night, or the rush for the food bowl when dinner is served, in which it seems to be a case of every cat for himself. But even these behaviors have a part to play in establishing and maintaining social order. Each is an example of the type of winner-take-all situation that nature employs to ensure the survival of the fittest. By means of these, and a host of other contests, cats establish their own strict hierarchy which, by giving each animal a clearly defined part to play within the group, sustains the social structure.

The Role of the Male

In a typical cat colony there is a clear difference between the rather loose-knit social hierarchy among females, which is based on the number of litters produced, and that of toms, where each is carefully ranked according to his rating on a kind of animal macho scale. The more assertive their behavior, the higher status in the group.

Any new, unneutered male arriving in the neighborhood will immediately be challenged by high-ranking males of the pack into whose territory he has intruded. A series of fights takes place usually over several nights, in order to establish the newcomer's standing. Status struggles of this kind are the special interest of Dr. Charles Winslow at Brooklyn College's Department of Psychology. His portrait of the top cat in one of the colonies he studied is: "A swaggering and strutting male . . . from whom most of the other animals withdrew. He was not the largest animal . . . but possessed the 'cockiness' trait to such a degree that even a larger male was conspicuously sub-ordinate.''

When the group was offered food, this cat immediately rushed to claim it while the remaining animals hung back and made no attempt to approach him. Only when he had eaten his fill were other cats allowed to share the remains. Within the colony the other cats formed ranks according to their various degrees of dominance, although the social pattern was suppressed by the presence of this powerful and undisputed leader.

In order to discover whether dominance was associated with an animal's sex, Dr. Winslow deliberately introduced strange cats, both males and females, one at a time into the group. The reaction of the top cat, the "swaggering strutting male," remained the same no matter what the newcomer's sex.

"He strutted and raised his back and tail in a more de fiant manner than at any other time, and approached the new animals. He would then seize each in turn by the loose flesh at the nape of the neck and push it back down with his own hindquarters and mount as in copulation." The unfortunate interloper was pushed flat on the floor as the dominant cat stood on its back, ignoring the victim's yowls of outrage and distress. Eventually the cowed newcomer was allowed to escape to the sanctuary of a shelf or win-dowsill, where it remained trembling and fearful for hours, even refusing to join the others when food arrived.

"During several days the attacks were very frequent," writes Dr. Winslow, "and the yowling of the subjected animals continual." The whole colony remained in an up-roar until, abruptly, the assaults declined in number and became only sporadic, by which time the newcomer had been completely subdued and subjugated.

Although it involved a parody of the sex act, Dr. Winslow was struck by the complete absence of any sexual component, either hetero- or homosexual, in the unequal contest. The assaulted animals never gave any signs of either enjoying or wanting to take part in the activity and escaped at the earliest possible moment. It was clear that the whole process was designed to demonstrate dominance on the part of the top cat and to produce a sufficient degree of submissiveness in the stranger. Once these two goals had been achieved, the newcomer was accepted into the colony and peace was restored.

Not one of the cats introduced to the colony by Dr. Winslow ever attempted to oust the established leader. There seemed to be a clear consensus about who ruled and this was communicated by other members of the pack to the interloper.

At one point during the observations, however, the top cat fell ill and had to be removed for treatment. In his absence, changes gradually occurred in the colony's behavior. For a while all the cats shared food equally and seemed subdued. After a short time, however, the next most assertive cat started to become more assertive and his bearing grew increasingly dominant, although he rarely felt the need to attack other members of the group in order to demonstrate just who was boss.

The cat pack, especially in the wild, is ruled by a single tom. The more dominant he is, the larger the territory over which he is allowed to reign as undisputed despot, although the extent of his domain and the degree of dominance does not necessarily provide an indication of the number of females with whom he will be able to mate. Furthermore, dominance tends to be restricted to a particular area. A cat who commands complete obedience within his territory may act submissively when in unfamiliar surroundings. Fights, during which status is challenged or a new arrival initiated into the group, typically take place over several nights, but once a tom has been allocated a rank in the hierarchy, he is only likely to have a fight again in special circumstances: when taking part in the "blooding" of a newcomer, if challenging for a high status in the group or when challenged himself by a socially ambitious animal.

Although cat fights sound terrifyingly brutal, like most disputes between wild animals they are generally more symbolic than serious and contain a great deal of ritualized aggression whose function is to establish a winner without putting the survival of either animal seriously at risk. While spitting and snarling, the contestants are careful to aim most of their blows at the head and neck regions, which are well protected against such assaults. When ears get nicked or eyes are injured, it's usually the result of a tom fighting a stronger or more cunning opponent, a complete accident or a momentary lapse in that animal's defense.

Toms also fight outside the house of a receptive female for the chance to mate with her, but ethologists generally view such contests as squabbles over territory rather than struggles for the female's favors. After the tumult has ceased, a loser has just as much chance of being chosen by the female as the winner, who will not usually do anything to oppose her decision.

When a tom has been neutered, he gradually slips down the hierarchy and may even end up as one of the colony's outcasts, pariah cats who, acting as feline scapegoats, receive the wrath of every other cat in the group and are consistently being abused and assaulted.

However, unlike humans and monkeys, cats do not have a complete dominant-submissive hierarchy where, for example, A punishes B, who punishes C, and so on down the line. Only one cat rules the roost and his will dominates all the remainder who, with the exception of outcast cats, all share equal rank below him.

But being top cat brings duties as well as status. His task is to safeguard females in the colony from the attention of outsiders and to protect their domain against the pillage of its food stocks. He is also intensely loyal to the pack, thus helping them all survive. Cats lower in rank to the leader are usually assigned guard duty and charged with the task of driving out any intruders.

The Role of the Female

Among feral and wild cats, the basic social unit is the mother and kitten, with some males deputized into paternal roles. The hierarchy among females is determined by the number of litters produced, the greater the number, the higher being the social standing of that queen. A mother with kittens, however, outranks all other females while she is weaning them. Females cooperate to a considerable extent in raising their litters, taking it in turns to watch over the kittens or bring food to nursing mothers. When several queens give birth at the same time, families may be amalgamated so that they can share out such chores as feeding, grooming and playing with the young. Experienced mothers often help first-timers, especially when the birth is difficult. They have been seen cutting the umbilical cord with their teeth and licking clean the latest arrivals.

A great deal that humans do—often with the best of intentions—has a disruptive effect on this complicated social structure. For example, a female who has been spayed after the birth of a litter loses considerable social standing, but one neutered before she has even come into heat is unlikely ever to establish herself in the colony and may be forced into lonely isolation.

As I have mentioned already, neutered toms drop quickly in status, so whenever public pressure leads to campaigns for neutering all stray animals before returning them to the wild it is essential to bear in mind the need to preserve a few entire males to assume the role of leaders.

The social life of the domestic cat is often very different from that of his wild cousins. Bearing in mind that some 70 percent of all the toms in any pet community will have been neutered before reaching maturity, and given the high density of cats in urban communities, it is hardly surprising that their society should undergo marked changes.

They are far more tolerant of one another than in the wild, and establish "neutral" zones between their territories on which meetings can be arranged without threat of combat. Territories are carefully marked out, and shared pathways organized if the lie of the land makes this a necessity. When using these communal routes, the cats are careful to avoid one another, checking visually and through the use of smells whether the way is clear. If a confrontation does occur by chance, rather than fight over the right of way the cats will sit and stare at one another. Frequently the more timid of the two eventually loses his nerve and leaves the area, but if both eyeball it out there is likely to be a sharp increase in aggression signals until one decides that enough is enough and gives ground. Victory in such encounters does not, however, bestow any status on the winner, who is quite likely to come off worst in any subsequent clash.

The disruption of their social groups and the importance of human beings in their lives means that cats have to adjust in other ways as well. Usually this involves regarding their owner as a member of the group and responding toward him or her exactly as they would toward another cat.

Does Your Cat Really Care?

If you feed and show affection toward a cat, it will respond to such attentions with its own brand of tender loving care. It will feel an obligation toward you, as a member of the pack, and often an intense loyalty both to its owner and the home base. As we have seen, so powerful is this emotional tie that cats are prepared to travel thousands of miles in order to be reunited with their former families.

While it is unlikely that cats, or any other animals, are capable of the depth and complexity of human emotions, affectionate behavior such as head-rubbing, grooming and what might be called "cuddling" is often observed between male-female pairs in colonies. The last activity involves a pair sitting beside one another with cheeks pressed together, heads pointing in the same direction, an affectionate pose they will hold for many minutes. This is especially likely after the female has produced their kittens.

Cats frequently exchange friendly greetings by taking it in turns to offer their heads for sniffing. Next they walk slowly past one another, rubbing their raised heads together, just once or several times in rapid succession, before the two either sit down and blink affectionately at each other or lie down with their bodies in close contact.

Similar responses are also directed toward those who care for them, especially nuzzling and lip-rubbing to establish ownership over that person.

Cats also have an instinctive need to protect their home base against many types of threat, as Terry Fackrell, his wife Christine and their two sons Wayne and Stephen discovered after a fire broke out, late one night, in the living room of their Bristol home.

Christine was sound asleep when Zoe, their Siamese cat, rushed up the stairs, jumped onto her face and started scratching her urgently. Realizing that something was wrong, Christine got up, discovered the fire and raised the alarm. Thanks to Zoe, the whole family escaped uninjured from the badly damaged building. So impressed were the local firemen that they gave Zoe a special "bravery award," two cans of her favorite fish.

The Hunting Cat

Cats bring gifts of food to those who feed them by way of repayment for kindness received, but why, owners often wonder, should these unpleasant relics be left in such inappropriate places as an unmade bed, a pile of clothes or a favorite armchair? The simple answer is that the cat chooses the locations because anything which humans use frequently carries their odor very strongly. This, to the cat's way of thinking, means it is very likely that the owner will return to the same spot and so be sure to find their offering.

It is both futile and cruel to scold or punish your cat for this activity, which is deeply ingrained in its evolutionary heritage. In human terms, it's the equivalent of slapping your best friend in the face merely because he has given you a nice birthday present. If you choose to own a cat, you must accept that this involves sharing your life with a predator whose hunting instincts are an indelible product of its genetic makeup.

Owners sometimes protest that there is no need for their pet to kill animals, since he is always so well fed. But this argument shows a misunderstanding of how the various instinctive needs of the cat are regulated. Feeding, hunting and fighting behaviors are controlled by different areas of the brain, which means that a full stomach will do little to reduce the cat's desire to stalk and to kill. Once a young cat has sampled the delights of the hunt, this activity quickly becomes so rewarding that it may develop into a major component of its repertoire of behavior. Once this has happened, the need is so deeply ingrained that retraining is seldom possible.

Apart from keeping your cat a prisoner at home twenty-four hours a day, there is little to be done to prevent the hunt and avoid its—to many humans—unpleasant consequences. It certainly helps if you pick a kitten, weaned at around six weeks, from a mother who never showed any interest in hunting. Conversely, of course, if you are getting a cat to keep down rats and mice, always choose a kitten from the litter of a female who is herself an enthusiastic hunter.

It is also possible to discourage kittens from stalking and killing birds, for example, by early training. The procedure advocated by several breeders is to use a toy bird and a water pistol. Fix the bird up in the garden at the end of a piece of string so that you can make it move while staying concealed some distance away. As the kitten starts stalking your decoy, move the bird slightly to make it look more lifelike. As he pounces, squirt him with the water pistol. This doesn't do any harm, but it gives the cat a nasty surprise. After a few such shocks, any desire to stalk and kill birds could well subside. It is important when doing this to remain out of sight so that the cat doesn't come to link any behavior on your part with the punishment.

Even if your cat is a hunter, there is no need to feel especially upset or guilty, or to imagine that his activities will seriously reduce the local bird population. Most birds manage to get away from the cat, and even those that are caught and killed make up less than 25 percent of the average cat's hunting trophies. You may also find some comfort in the fact that cats are extremely well-equipped to dispatch their victims swiftly and usually with little pain.

Killing is done by means of a single bite to the nape of the neck, the slight depression between skull and body acting as a visual stimulus which triggers this response. As the jaws close, two long canine teeth slip like rapier blades between the bones of the spine, severing the spinal cord and causing instant death. Experienced cats kill more efficiently than young and untutored animals who, like the novice matador, may blunder before finding just the right spot to administer the *coup de grâce*. Cats' whiskers also play an important part in identifying the correct spot for the death bite, which means that animals who have suffered damage to these important sense organs are unlikely to be able to hunt and kill with the same speed and accuracy as before their injury.

Rats and mice sometimes hunch up their shoulders when captured to make the bite impossible. To disorientate its prey, the cat must therefore toss it violently to one side before pouncing again in the hope of being able to accomplish the kill. Larger rodents, such as rats, may be beaten with the paws to subdue them. These actions give rise to the idea that the cat is being wantonly cruel and playing with its victims. But even the behavior which seems much more like sadistic teasing, such as letting a victim make an apparently successful escape attempt before pouncing once again, must be seen in terms of the cat's inborn need constantly to practice and perfect its hunting or trapping skills.

Why Cats Need Space Around Them

Body language specialists are said to amuse themselves at dull parties by performing what they have nicknamed the "cocktail two-step," a subtle exploitation of nonverbal communication which works as follows. The victim chosen is someone who prefers to keep people at arm's length while talking. Stand too close and he or she immediately backs off to maintain a certain distance between you.

Slowly and carefully, the person playing the cocktail two-step invades his companion's "no-go" zone, obliging the victim to shuffle backwards in order to reestablish his body space. By gradually invading his territory again, a further retreat is achieved. It is said that some experts are able to maneuver a suitable victim right around the room and back to the starting point without the person ever being aware of what's happening!

This game provides a good illustration of the need, which everybody has in varying degrees, to keep a certain distance from others, to maintain a personal space which becomes part of our physical being and whose uninvited violation leads to the distressing feeling that one's privacy is under attack.

The amount of personal space required varies according to the circumstances of an encounter and our relationship with the person. Most people feel uncomfortable when strangers stray closer than three feet, for example, although friends can come within eighteen inches without making us uneasy. Intimate partners, of course, come even closer.

Cats too have a need for a personal space around them, although their behavior here can be puzzling. On some occasions a cat will insist on keeping a certain distance between himself and others and even seem affronted if a human trespasses on his invisible domain. At other times, the same cat may crave physical contact, with other cats or his owner, and will spend hours snuggled against another's body.

Roger Tabor, author of *The Wildlife of the Domestic Cat*, says that the amount of personal space demanded by cats living in colonies gives an excellent indication of the time they have spent together and the amount of affection between them. When a group has only recently been established, the individuals steer well clear of one another, five yards from their neighbor while feeding and at least two yards during the remainder of the time. Should a cat venture into another's personal space, the response will either be threat calls and displays of aggression or a rapid retreat.

When cats have known one another for a reasonable amount of time, however, this desire to keep their distance declines until they are happy to share the same meal dish and snuggle close to one another while resting. When observing groups of strays, therefore, always make a special point of noting how much space they choose to leave between each other and you will have an excellent guide as to how long that colony has been formed.

In the mid-1970s one of the most extensive studies of feral cats was carried out by two British researchers, David McDonald and Peter Apps. They spent months observing a well-established colony whose base was a farm in the quiet Devon countryside. These animals knew one another so well that there was no question of any wanting to keep their distance. Even when asleep, cat companions liked to rest close to one another, often making bodily contact with their friends while sleeping, just as pets often do with their human owners during the night

Cats of both sexes seem to have this strong need for physical contact. A male, for example, will sometimes take over from the female after the litter has been born, curling his body around the kittens and protecting some of them with his front paws, a position he is usually quite happy to adopt for an hour or more. Kittens are an exception to this distance rule. Like human infants, they often engage in uninhibited displays of affection or periods of unrestrained rough-and-tumble play.

Pets have a far less powerful desire for personal space

than do wild or feral cats, and it is quite common to see two domesticated cats respond with mutual friendly interest at the first meeting.

How Smells Help Cat Society

Apart from the special chemicals, pheromones, which establish ownership over objects or people and the boundary of a cat's territory, there is another use of smell which plays a vital part in regulating cat society. This is the habit of spraying, undertaken by male cats, with a carefully directed stream of pungent liquid, against some landmark such as a tree stump, post or large stone which has a special significance for the cat. This scent, which, unlike other pheromones, is all too easily detected by humans, does more than merely mark territorial boundaries. By varying the amount produced, and causing subtle changes in the odor, cats are able to communicate information about their age, status and even their identity.

Recently I made a comparison between dominance and the relation of other animals to spray. When an animal was high in rank, others took care to avoid the sprayed area. This happened far less frequently when the spray had been left by a cat of a more lowly status. In many cases, original spray markings are oversprayed by rival cats. This is a common occurrence and probably indicates that the second animal feels more macho than the first. In those cases where the original sprayer noticed what happened, he immediately made a rush at the intruder, usually frightening him off, although there were occasions when a fight ensued.

Neutering reduces the male's desire to spray, although he may well do so occasionally, especially when feeling stressed, and this is sometimes a consideration when owners are wondering whether or not a visit to the vet is called for. Cats will also spray when they feel their territory is being threatened, for instance if several animals inhabit the same house. However, it is often possible to reduce the amount of spraying inside the house by the simple expedient of feeding the animal in areas where you are anxious he should not perform this activity. Cats seldom spray in areas where they eat, so this offers at least some protection. Punishing the cat is futile, although many inexperienced owners do this in the mistaken belief that the cat's house training is at fault. Spray does not have anything to do with a desire to empty the bladder.

Cats often display a sense of ownership about the territory they inhabit which, at times, borders on the obsessional, and constantly mark it using a variety of bodily products, including feces, urine, excretions from the anal glands, saliva and ear secretions. These are investigated by other animals using both their normal sense of smell and the *flehmen* response. Sometimes the reaction will be to overlay the scent, by spraying, rubbing his chin or mouth against it, or in some other manner. Alternatively, the cat may start to roll vigorously on the ground, rubbing his body with great intensity over the marked area. Cats tend to do this when they encounter the scent left by one of their friends, and may later go to sleep on this spot. Indoors the preference may lead your cat to seek out some of your old clothes or to curl up on an unmade bed, often in preference to a far more comfortable sleeping basket. This shows that he regards you as a friendly member of his colony and finds your smell comforting and relaxing. Some cats, when detecting the underarm odor of their owners on discarded clothes, will engage in extremely vigorous rolling and rubbing in much the same way that they do when presented with catnip, or catmint, a weed found in Europe and North America whose scent is especially attractive to cats. Only about 50 percent of all cats are affected by it (and the tendency appears to be inherited), but those that are go into a form of trance which can last for up to fifteen minutes. The active ingredient, nepetalactone, stimulates the same pathways in the brain as LSD and marijuana, suggesting that the state of intense pleasure induced is akin to a human's drug trip.

The picture that emerges, then, is of an animal which, left to its own devices, creates an elaborate and carefully organized social life whose purpose is to promote the survival of the colony as a whole. For this purpose cats have evolved a large number of ritual activities, from establishing dominance to displays of affection, and learned to mark out their territory in such a way that animals from different colonies can use the same terrain for hunting or mating at different times. They also leave neutral ground between different territories so as to have a place where meetings can take place without the risk of hostilities.

Females are excellent mothers and cooperate with one another in the rearing of kittens. They are quick to sense danger, and capable of carrying their young considerable distances to safety when any threat arises.

When cats are owned by humans, the person responsible for feeding them is quickly accepted as a member of the pack and is often the recipient of well-intended if rather revolting tributes.

The more we discover about the private life of the cat, the greater our respect should be for their well-ordered and organized society. Yet it is a social life even now under threat in most parts of the Western world, and one which could soon vanish for ever. Selective breeding and the increasing domestication of cats may well lead to a species in which many of the old, instinctive drives have been either repressed or lost entirely.

But a loss of the desire to live in groups may not be the only skill which is being bred out of them as cats become increasingly remote from their wild ancestors. Indeed, it is possible that many of the incredible talents which I have described in this book could, before too long, be no more than a memory.

At the moment, however, there remains an excellent chance that many will still be present in your own pet.

CHAPTER 10

Exploring Your Cat's Secret Powers

While it seems certain that all cats possess the remarkable powers described in the previous chapters, many of these inborn talents are seldom used and rarely revealed. A possible explanation for this neglect can be found in the animal's increasing domestication which, together with selective breeding, makes some of its natural abilities less important and less potent. These skills are, however, latent rather than lost, and may be called upon by the cat whenever a serious need arises.

Over the past years scientists have developed a number of techniques for assessing such hidden talents, and I have used some of their findings in creating the eight tests which follow. These will allow you to investigate your cat's psychic powers, measure key aspects of his IQ and assess his personality.

Since several of these tests involve a food reward, it is best to try them out just before normal meal times when the cat's appetite is likely to be at its peak. In most instances you have to repeat the assessments on a number of occasions, and these should be spread over several days to avoid boredom on both your parts. A lack of motivation, in either you or the animal, will make it far harder to uncover these skills.

Make sure that the atmosphere is relaxed and happy during each test, since most cats are extremely sensitive to human mood. As we saw in the chapter on extrasensory perception, the cats who did best in the maze test were those who had been treated with affection in the period immediately prior to the experiment, while those who were in any way emotionally distressed performed extremely poorly. Never become impatient with your cat if he fails to do what you hoped for. Simply postpone the assessment for a time when you are both in a better mood.

Let's start by looking at three ways of investigating your cat's extrasensory perception. If your cat is "left-pawed," the chances are good that he possesses psychic ability to some extent, although you must not be too disappointed if, despite this hopeful sign, you are unable to discover any paranormal powers.

Can Cats Read Your Mind?

Test 1

This is an extremely simple test to perform and one which can be carried out at almost any time, since the only equipment needed is a watch with a sweep second hand or digital readout. Although rapid and easy to administer, it has been employed by several leading psychic researchers and yielded excellent results. Between 15 and 20 percent of the cats assessed in this way have been found to possess some degree of telepathic ability.

HOW TO DO IT

The best time to try this test is while your cat is sitting, not lying, down. His front legs should be completely straight with his hindquarters placed firmly on the ground. In this position he is most likely to be reasonably relaxed, but still sufficiently alert to pick up a telepathic message. He should be facing away from you, with his head turned between 90 and 120 degrees, making it impossible for him even to glimpse your expression or posture, both of which could provide clues which would interfere with the test.

If the cat is looking in the wrong direction, shift your own position rather than attempting to move him, since this inevitably increases his alertness and research suggests that an aroused cat is far less receptive to ESP signals than a relaxed one.

Sit down, make yourself comfortable, unwind physically and clear your mind. Let your thoughts dwell on some pleasantly tranquil image, perhaps a quiet country scene or a soothing color. At first you may find it difficult to banish distracting ideas from your mind, but this will come with a little practice.

Once you feel mentally and physically at ease, glance at your watch to obtain the starting time and then stare hard at your cat for exactly ten seconds. It is essential not to make any movement or sound at this stage to avoid attracting his attention by other than telepathic means.

Focus your mind as intensely as possible on some shared and pleasurable experience, a friendly game or a session of affectionate petting which you both enjoyed. Try to beam this impression across the room to your cat. If he turns and stares at you during the ten seconds in which this mind message is being transmitted, note that success by placing a tick on a sheet of paper.

Over the next few days or weeks, repeat this test on a further nineteen occasions, varying the time of day at which it is carried out. This is important because investigations have found that ESP seems to be stronger in some people during the evening and more powerful in others first thing in the morning. These changes seem likely to be due to the body's natural circadian rhythms and the biochemical changes which they bring about in the functioning of mind and body.

Every head turn during the ten-second telepathy test period results in a tick on the record form. When all twenty trials have been completed, count the number of ticks and use the chart below to obtain your cat's ESP rating on this test.

Number of successes	Psychic power revealed
0–2	No telepathic ability
3–5	Slight ability shown
6–8	Moderate ESP present
9–12	High level of psi ability
12+	Phenomenal!

If you obtained a score of 3 or more on Test 1, it will certainly be worthwhile attempting the second assessment, which involves a slightly tougher test of ESP.

Even if your cat showed no signs of being able to read your mind on Test 1, however, it may prove worthwhile exploring this alternative approach, as cats who fail on one form of testing sometimes show surprisingly good results when assessed in other ways.

Test 2—Finding Food Through ESP*

WHAT YOU NEED

For this test you require two feeding dishes and two plastic containers that can be used to cover them completely. As it is important to achieve a good seal between the edges of the covers and the floor, the assessment is best done on linoleum or something similar rather than on a carpet.

If you feel like improving on the basic method, an electric fan will be needed, but this is not an essential requirement.

HOW TO DO IT

Step One: Place a scrap of food on one of the dishes and cover both with the plastic containers. Now attract your cat toward the plates with another tidbit. When he reaches the covered dishes, remove the cover from the one which has the food in it and allow the cat to claim the reward. Repeat this process until the cat learns to go straight up to the correct dish and either tries to push off the container or meows for you to remove it. Most cats learn this within a couple of sessions.

Step Two: When the cat goes straight to the food, switch the tidbit to the other dish. As he approaches the plate that used to hold the snack, lift off the cover and show him it's empty. Next, gently turn his head toward the second plate, raise the container to reveal the reward and allow him to eat it. Repeat this several times until the cat has shifted his attention to the second dish.

*I have adapted this assessment from experimental work funded by the Rockefeller Foundation and carried out by Drs. Karlis Osis and Esther Foster at the Duke University Parapsychology Laboratory.

Step Three: Start moving the food randomly between the two plates, without letting him see you do so. While this confuses the cat at first, he quickly learns that the snack may be hidden under either cover. Once this lesson has been mastered, you are ready to start the ESP test itself.

Step Four: Put the cat about ten feet away from the covered dishes and looking toward them. Restrain him for ten seconds while you focus your thoughts on the dish which contains the food, but avoid looking at it directly, since this will give him too much of a clue. Concentrate hard and then release him. As he walks toward the covers, continue to think hard about the correct dish.

If your cat chooses successfully, lift the cover and allow him to eat. Note this outcome by making a tick on the record sheet. As with the previous test, repeat this procedure to make a total of twenty times over a period of days or weeks and vary the time of day, sometimes testing him before the morning feed, sometimes in the evening or last thing at night.

Switch the food from dish to dish randomly by tossing a coin to choose which will contain the reward. You might decide, for example, that if it's heads you will put the snack on the right-hand dish and on the left dish if it lands tails.

Clearly, any odor escaping under the covers would offer the cat a major clue as to which dish to select—remember that he has an extremely keen sense of smell. Provided the containers rest evenly on the floor, this should not prove a problem, although you can introduce an additional safeguard by positioning an electric fan behind the cat so that any scent of the food is carried away from him.

On each test, the odds of him picking the correct dish by chance alone are, of course, 50-50, which means he must make the right choice on more than ten occasions before you can read anything significant into the results.

Number of correct choices	Psychic power
11–12	Moderate
13–15	Good
15+	Excellent

If you obtained a score much below 10, then some of the *reverse* telepathy seems to be occurring, with your mental images actually preventing him from making a random selection. If this happens, you could experiment by using different images to see whether the success rate increases.

Test 3—Calling Your Cat by Telepathy

This assessment is probably only worth attempting if you have discovered an above-average level of psychic communication between you, and of course it is likely to be affected by the closeness of your relationship with your cat and how obedient he is to the spoken command. The idea is to call the cat to you purely by means of telepathy.

Start by attempting to send a "come here" signal when your cat is in a room nearby. Relax and then focus your mind on the *image* of the cat running to greet you. Hold this as vividly as possible for ten seconds. Now wait another ten seconds to see if the cat appears. If he does, record this success in the usual way. Repeat on nineteen further occasions and only proceed to the next stage if the cat comes at your telepathic summons on five or more occasions.

If you have no success at first, try varying the mental pictures being used to attract the cat to your side. You might, for instance, concentrate on the image of him being fed, and picture yourself placing a dish of his favorite food on the floor as he comes running eagerly over.

If you achieve success in a summons between rooms, you may be encouraged to attempt the more difficult task of calling the cat over a greater distance, perhaps from upstairs or in from the garden.

The further away he is, the more time you must allow for him to rejoin you. But it rarely pays to attempt to transmit the telepathic command for longer than ten seconds since, especially at first, it is hard to focus clearly on a particular image for much longer.

If your cat does obey an ESP command, reward him immediately with warm praise and a tidbit. That way you encourage and strengthen any latent psychic powers he may possess. But never become annoyed or impatient with him if there is no response. It could be that you are not sending a powerful enough message or that he was distracted by something more exciting when it arrived.

Once psychic communications have been established, however, you should find it possible to summon your cat over considerable distances.

Number of successful calls	ESP Rating
5–8	Slight
9–11	Moderate
12+	High

If you discovered a psychic link between you, then enhance this by frequent practice. As with any other ability, *psi* powers need to be used regularly in order to develop fully and function efficiently.

Now let's move into an area where results seem likely

to owe as much to the cat's well-developed natural senses
as to any psychic ability.

Does Your Cat Foretell the Future?

Test 4

To carry out this assessment you simply need to observe your
cat closely for a few weeks and keep a written note of the
different things he does, together with the details of the times
of day and places where they occurred, for example:

10 A.M.	Six minutes of vigorous grooming in front room.
11 A.M.	Begged to be allowed out.
11:30 A.M.	Returned and fell asleep on window ledge.
1:15 P.M.	Ate dinner.
1:30 P.M.	Climbed to top of bookshelf, seemed afraid for no real reason.

After two weeks of observations, you will have collected
a large amount of information about his behavior. The next
task is to rate each activity's degree of unusualness, as
follows:

1+ Very common; carries out this activity almost
every day.

2+ Fairly common; does this on at least three days
of the week.

3+ Slightly less common; seen occasionally.

4+ Very uncommon; only observed a few times.

5+ Rarely seen.

The purpose of this initial two weeks of observation is to collect background information about your cat's habits. You will probably not find any behaviors which merit a rating of 5 and, by definition, few which deserve a score of 4.

In the list of observations above, for example, grooming, begging to go out and eating dinner might rate a 1; sleeping on the window ledge could be rated as 2; while climbing onto the bookshelf might score 3, 4 or even 5.

Once you have gathered these basic data, you should ignore anything that comes into categories 1 or 2, take a little more notice of activities rated 3, and pay close attention to those actions which are sufficiently infrequent to gain a rating of 4 or 5.

When your cat behaves in this exceptional manner, make a note of anything out of the ordinary which happens, either in your home or close by. Such events could include:

A bereavement

The return of a relative after a long period

An unexpected visitor

Good news

Bad news

An accident to a member of the family

The birth of a baby

A natural disaster in the immediate vicinity, such as a flood, forest fire, earth tremor, thunder storm with lightning damage, blizzard, heat wave or torrential downpour.

By discovering a link between what your cat does and what subsequently happens, it becomes possible to foretell, at least to some extent, what the future holds. You may be able to predict especially bad weather, for example, purely through an association with your cat's strange behavior.

Assessing Your Cat's IQ

Intelligence in humans comprises several related mental skills and it seems almost certain that the same applies to cats, which is why I have included three tests which assess different aspects of their intellectual ability. If you own a cat and a dog, you might like to try them on both animals to see which is the smarter.

Test 5—How Fast Does Your Cat Learn?

The rate at which fresh skills are mastered or new information learned is an important aspect of human IQ. If the animal experts are right in believing that cats could soon find work in the home and on the factory floor, then this aspect of their intelligence will become increasingly significant.

WHAT YOU NEED

The only apparatus required is a hoop, about two feet in diameter. Use a child's toy or construct one from a stiff plastic tube formed into a circle and held with a wooden peg.

HOW TO DO IT

The object is to teach your cat to jump through the hoop and note how many trials it takes for him to perfect this trick. Start by positioning the hoop about one foot from the ground while holding a tempting tidbit in the other hand. Display the snack at the midpoint of the hoop, and just within the circle.

Now say firmly: "Come on!" and indicate the reward by moving your hand slightly. Initially the cat will probably just raise himself on his hind legs and grab the food, which you should allow him to eat.

When he has learned to rise up for the reward, move to the next part of the training by drawing the food back through the hoop and encouraging him to follow. If he tries to run around the side to get a reward, push him gently but firmly back.

Remember to say, "Come on" each time you present the reward and to keep a note of the number of times this command is given, since your cat's score on this test consists of the total instructions which have to be given before the lesson has been mastered.

The final stage of training consists of holding up the hoop and calling out, "Come on" without showing the cat any food. Just extend your hand as if offering a reward and give the command. The idea is to link this instruction with the desired action so firmly that the words alone are sufficient to produce an eager leap. If he jumps correctly, you can then provide a tidbit taken from a container which is kept well away from the hoop.

The test is completed when the cat jumps through the hoop correctly on at least two out of three occasions. Now rate his IQ using the chart below:

Number of commands given	IQ rating
60+	Below average
50–60	Slightly below average

40–49	Average
30–39	Above average
29 or less	Very intelligent

As you can see, a very large number of attempts may be needed before the cat masters this trick, so it is essential to spread the training over several days, allowing him a rest day between each practice session. Keep these sessions short and hold them immediately prior to mealtimes so that the food has maximum appeal.

Test 6—How Skilled Is Your Cat at Choosing?

The next test explores what is called "discrimination learning," that is, the ability to make a logical choice between two alternatives. It is an important aspect of intelligence and one at which some cats excel.*

WHAT YOU NEED

Two pieces of string about two feet long, a table and two sheets of cardboard. One should be in the shape of a square, about four inches across, and the other cut into a circle of four inches diameter.

HOW TO DO IT

Tie a piece of string to each square and circle, then suspend them from the table so that the shapes hang about six inches above the ground. Select either one of them—it doesn't matter which—for use as the target and persuade the cat to

*The procedure described has been adapted from a test standard developed by Dr. J. Warren of the Psychology Department at Stanford University and Dr. A. Barron of Oregon University.

begin a game with it by swinging the shape and encouraging him to bat it with a paw. As soon as he does so, reward him with food.

Continue in this way until he has learned to bat at that one specific shape in order to receive the snack. Change the position of these shapes every so often so that neither always hangs to either the left or the right, otherwise the cat may be discriminating on this basis rather than from a choice of shapes.

Note the number of times that he makes a mistake and bats the wrong shape in the hope of being rewarded. Continue with the training until he bats the target shape on four out of five occasions.

Number of errors	Learning skill shown
45+	Low
35–40	Slightly below average
30–34	Average
25–29	Slightly above average
24 or less	Good

Test 7—Is Your Cat Colorblind?

There has always been some disagreement among experts about whether cats can perceive colors, so here's an interesting variation on the above assessment which you might like to try. It will not only allow you to explore different aspects of your pet's talent for discrimination learning but could also reveal which colors he can see most clearly.

Modify the experiment by using two squares of identical size but different colors. Select colors which are equally bright to avoid providing a clue based on tones rather than colors. You might, for instance, start by working with a red and a yellow, then try a blue and a green.

Proceed exactly as before and count the number of errors until the cat has learned which of the colored squares must be batted to obtain a reward. Naturally you must switch them around, as before, or the cat will soon discriminate between left and right rather than on the basis of color. Use the same score chart as for Test 6.

Assessing Your Cat's Personality

Every cat possesses certain characteristics of personality and temperament which make him a unique individual. You probably have a strong feeling about the kind of creature your pet really is, but might still like to know how his personality compares with that of other cats.

All you have to do is to answer the twenty questions below, either from your knowledge of the animal or by observing him in different situations during the next few days or weeks. The score chart will then suggest the key personality variables.

I have also included a second assessment for your own use. By comparing the results, it should then be possible to find out how well-suited you are to one another on key aspects of personality.

Test 8—Cat's Personality Assessment

Circle whichever answer reflects the way your cat behaves in the situations described.

1. My cat runs to greet me when I come home after a short absence.
   a) Always.   b) Occasionally.   c) Seldom or never.

2. My cat enjoys playing with other cats.
   a) Always. b) Occasionally. c) Seldom or never.

3. My cat likes to be petted.
   a) Always. b) Occasionally. c) Seldom or never.

4. My cat frightens easily.
   a) Seldom or never. b) Occasionally. c) Always.

5. When strangers visit the house, my cat makes a fuss of them.
   a) Always. b) Occasionally. c) Seldom or never.

6. My pet makes the first approaches when meeting another cat.
   a) Always. b) Occasionally. c) Seldom or never.

7. My cat eats wholesome but unfamiliar food with relish.
   a) Always. b) Occasionally. c) Seldom or never. ·

8. If taken to unfamiliar surroundings, my cat starts exploring his new home soon after arriving.
   a) Always. b) Occasionally. c) Seldom or never.

9. After a long journey, my cat settles down quickly.
   a) Always. b) Occasionally. c) Seldom or never.

10. My cat likes to sleep on my bed at night.
    a) Always. b) Occasionally. c) Seldom or never.

11. My cat is an enthusiastic hunter.
    a) Always. b) Occasionally. c) Seldom or never.

12. My cat likes to hide away in a quiet corner.
    a) Seldom or never. b) Occasionally. c) Frequently.

13. My cat becomes upset by any change in routine.
    a) Seldom or never. b) Occasionally. c) Frequently.

14. My cat soon gets bored with being petted.
    a) Seldom or never. b) Occasionally. c) Frequently.

15. My cat fights with other cats.
    a) Always. b) Occasionally. c) Seldom or never.

16. My cat seems restless and moody for no apparent reason.

a) Frequently. b) Occasionally. c) Rarely or never.

17. My cat strays from home.

a) Frequently. b) Occasionally. c) Seldom or never.

18. My cat enjoys rough-and-tumble games.

a) Frequently. b) Occasionally. c) Seldom or never.

19. My cat sulks if he doesn't get his own way.

a) Rarely or never. b) Occasionally. c) Frequently.

20. If scolded or punished, my cat becomes very upset.

a) Seldom or never. b) Occasionally. c) Frequently.

HOW TO SCORE

Award 3 points for each a) answer circled, 2 for every b) and 1 for each c) response.

Test 9—Owner's personality assessment

1. Do you enjoy traveling to countries you've never visited before?

a) Very much. b) To some extent. c) Not at all.

2. Do you enjoy lively parties?

a) Very much. b) To some extent. c) Not at all.

3. Do you find it easy to make new friends?

a) Usually. b) Occasionally. c) Seldom or never.

4. Do you stand up for yourself in an argument?

a) Always. b) Now and then. c) Seldom or never.

5. Do you like meeting new people?

a) Very much. b) To some extent. c) Not at all.

6. Would you consider yourself ambitious?

a) Very much. b) To some extent. c) Not at all.

7. Do you tend to worry about the future?

a) Rarely or never. b) Occasionally. c) Frequently.

8. Do you make a fuss if you get bad service in a restaurant?

   a) Always. b) Sometimes. c) Seldom or never.

9. Do you prefer to bottle up your emotions?

   a) Rarely or never. b) Occasionally. c) Most of the time.

10. Do you make the first move in starting a new relationship?

    a) Always. b) Usually. c) Seldom or never.

11. Can you talk openly about your feelings?

    a) Always. b) Occasionally. c) Seldom or never.

12. Does life seem too slow?

    a) Always. b) Occasionally. c) Seldom or never.

13. Does being the center of attention embarrass you?

    a) Not at all. b) To some extent. c) Very much.

14. Do you become tense and anxious in unfamiliar situations?

    a) Not at all. b) To some extent. c) Very much.

15. Would you avoid an argument rather than stand up for your rights?

    a) Never. b) Now and then. c) Almost always.

16. Do you apologize for things which are not really your fault?

    a) Rarely or never. b) Now and then. c) Fairly frequently.

17. Does routine get you down?

    a) Very much so. b) Occasionally. c) Rarely or never.

18. Do you think of yourself as an energetic person?

    a) Very much so. b) To some extent. c) Not really.

19. If you disagreed with somebody's view, would you say so?

    a) On most occasions. b) Rarely. c) Never.

20. Do you worry about your health?

    a) Seldom or never. b) Occasionally. c) Frequently.

Score in the same way as for the cat personality assessment.

WHAT THE SCORES REVEAL

SCORE:

20–30

Your cat's personality: Your pet appears to be rather shy and possibly slightly nervous in his approach to life. He probably prefers a quiet life in familiar surroundings to constant changes in routine.

He will be a very loyal and devoted companion who stays close to home and seldom worries you by straying.

Avoid scolding him too frequently or punishing him too severely, since your anger will distress him to a far greater extent than it would a more emotionally robust animal. Allow him to make the first advances when it comes to petting, as there will be frequent occasions when he wishes to be left alone, not from an absence of affection but just because he does not feel in the mood for too much contact.

35–45

Your cat is reasonably extroverted and energetic, although there will be occasions when he prefers his own company and finds too much attention overwhelming. Respect his wishes and try to adapt yourself to his moods. Avoid frequent changes in his routine or surroundings if you can, since these are likely to unsettle him more than you may realize.

45 +

Your cat seems a robust, lively and fairly extroverted creature who is perfectly capable of looking after himself and doesn't have much need for human companionship. There will, of course, be times when he is extremely affectionate, but you must also be prepared for times when he seems quite indifferent to your company and tends to treat home like an animal hotel. Don't be too hurt by such a cavalier attitude, however, since it is in his nature to be independent in behavior and outlook. Among the neighborhood cats he is likely to enjoy a high status and command their respect.

HOW WELL WILL YOU GET ALONG?

The higher your score on the assessment, the more independent, assertive and extroverted you are likely to be. Owners who score high (40+) are often irritated by the behavior of shy, retiring, and unassertive cats who obtain low marks on the assessment. Equally, those obtaining a lowish score may find high-scoring cats too independent. If you have been on bad terms with your cat, it could be because of such a personality clash.

Although extroverted humans do occasionally find themselves more attracted than annoyed by the passive, dependent love of an introverted pet, and while introverted owners can come to love and respect an active, extroverted feline loner, the chances are that a serious discrepancy between your personalities will lead to difficulties in the relationship. How problems are likely to arise is indicated by the following table. To use it, simply subtract the smaller score from the larger and note the difference.

Differences between two scores	How well you are matched
0–5	Very compatible. You should get along just fine.
6–10	There will be times when you get on one another's nerves, but not too many problems should arise.
11–20	The differences between your personalities are fairly large, which could lead to difficulties now and then.
20+	Opposites *do* attract, and it could well be that you enjoy a warm relationship despite your very different approaches to life. Yet if you find it hard to feel close to your cat on occasion and become irritated by his response, the real problem could be a clash of personalities.

CHAPTER 11

Incredible Cats

It was the arrival in Britain of plagues of grain-eating black rats, introduced by Crusaders returning from the Middle East, which first proved the cat's worth to the medieval inhabitants of this island. Then came the dark times, during the reigns of Mary Tudor and Elizabeth I, especially, when they were persecuted and executed as agents of Satan.

Today, happily, the cat's popularity is again on the increase and its value as a friend and companion has never been more apparent or more appreciated. Given cats' unique ability to help humans live healthier, happier and more secure lives, this is hardly surprising.

During the course of my investigations I was told a great many stories about cats, many of which emphasized their capacity for springing surprises on the human race. One of my favorites, recounted by a research scientist, perfectly illustrates the fact that where cats are concerned, even the experts can get caught out.

A professor of veterinary science at a leading British university owned a valuable white Persian of whom both he and his wife were extremely fond and proud. This cat had, however, one major flaw in his makeup: he simply hated traveling by train. The sight of a station, railway line or rolling stock was sufficient to send him into a furious passion, during which he would tear at his basket in a frantic attempt to escape.

One day the professor wanted to take his cat to visit relatives who lived some 400 miles away. Unwilling to drive all that distance, he decided to travel by train. Naturally he was extremely concerned about his cat's reactions to such a long rail journey.

His wife suggested that, on the way to the station, they should call in at his department, where one of the postgraduate students could give the animal a sedative to keep him calm on the trip. This they did and the student, without pausing to reflect too deeply on what he was doing, gave the animal an injection of a morphine-based drug.

With any other creature this would have been perfectly successful, but because the cat's nervous system functions in a unique way, the action of this powerful substance is not to tranquilize but to stimulate. As soon as he remembered this, the student began to panic, visualizing his superior struggling to handle a hyperactive and totally uncontrollable cat.

The professor returned from his holiday and the young man braced himself for a furious reprimand and even dismissal from the department. But days went by with nothing being said until, finally, the student decided he had to find out about the journey.

"My boy, it was a nightmare," sighed the professor.

"My cat broke out of its basket and raced up and down the train attacking passengers and railway staff."

Then, giving the man a grateful smile, he remarked: "Goodness only knows what would have happened if you hadn't tranquilized him!"

As I said, with cats one must never take *anything* for granted!

Index

About the Author

An expert in child development, **David Greene** first became interested in the study of cats when he noticed their beneficial effect on the youngsters with whom he was working. In particular, he found that children who owned cats appeared less prone to many emotional and social problems. Since that time, he has devoted years of research into gaining a better understanding of the ways in which cats are of benefit to humans. In addition to conducting psychological research, Greene runs a behavioral consultancy for families and industry. He lives in England.